PRAISE FOR *History of Rock 'n' Roll in Ten Songs*

"No writer puts you inside the experience of music the way Greil Marcus does. His descriptions of songs, especially, unfold like thrillers or romantic rhapsodies, sucking you in and revealing aspects of each beat or vocal trill that you'd never have noticed on your own. As the most esteemed music writer of his generation, Marcus has made a career of challenging conventional wisdom on everything from Elvis to punk to Bob Dylan's Basement Tapes. . . . It's so much fun to let him drag your brain onto the dance floor."—ANN POWERS, *NPR.com*

"For Marcus, every great song is a Rosetta Stone, an esoteric code. This approach gives him great imaginative, literary breadth. . . . Out of Marcus' dozen or so books, *Ten Songs* is the purest distillation of his ideas. . . . The chapters on Joy Division, on Buddy Holly, and on the two 'Money' songs are tours de force."—CARL WILSON, *Slate*

"Marcus is a man in brainy love with the music. I don't know of anyone else who writes as beautifully, and deeply, about songs and singing."—RODDY DOYLE, *Irish Times*

"What most matters to Marcus is rock 'n' roll as the site of a continuing conversation, a conversation between everyone who has performed or listened to this music, and between all its performances, past and still to come. *The History of Rock 'n' Roll in Ten Songs* is a magisterial contribution to this conversation."—SIMON FIRTH, *Product* magazine

"His accounts of listening to these songs, of being transported in unearthly directions by them, show him to be as bewitched by this music as he ever was. . . . *The Mystery of Rock 'n' Roll in Ten Songs* might have been a truer name for his latest inspired, wonder-struck book."—PAUL GENDERS, *TLS*

"Marcus is a great prose stylist, fun to read even when he's spinning his wheels, and often—there's no telling when—he will pick up speed and zoom off into unexpected territories."—EVAN KINDLEY, *Los Angeles Times*

"A stunning, virtuosic performance, as good as any and better than most of what Greil Marcus has written since 1975's genre-redefining *Mystery Train*. It's a hectic, wild and occasionally bumpy ride, loaded with trapdoors and wormholes leading to unexpected places where you never quite know who you'll confront next, and where you'll immediately yearn to hear every record to which he alludes."—CHARLES SHAAR MURRAY, *Literary Review*

"As emotional and intoxicatingly rich a troll's nest of rabbit holes as anything Greil Marcus has written since *Invisible Republic* or even *Lipstick Traces,* this is a book that deepens or refracts or turns on their heads a lot more than the ten songs (and the one history of the title)."—MARK SINKER, *The Wire*

"The book is really a series of essays, cunningly chiselled, lovingly woven, bold, tough and illuminating, the intention being 'to feel one's way through music as a field of expression and as a web of affinities.'"—MARK ELLEN, *New Statesman*

The History of Rock 'n' Roll
in Ten Songs

Also by Greil Marcus

Mystery Train: Images of America in Rock 'n' Roll Music (1975, 2008)

Lipstick Traces: A Secret History of the Twentieth Century (1989, 2009)

Dead Elvis: A Chronicle of a Cultural Obsession (1991)

In the Fascist Bathroom: Punk in Pop Music, 1977–1992 (1993, originally published as *Ranters & Crowd Pleasers*)

The Dustbin of History (1995)

The Old, Weird America: The World of Bob Dylan's Basement Tapes (2000, 2011, originally published as *Invisible Republic,* 1997)

Double Trouble: Bill Clinton and Elvis Presley in a Land of No Alternatives (2000)

"The Manchurian Candidate" (2002)

Like a Rolling Stone: Bob Dylan at the Crossroads (2005)

The Shape of Things to Come: Prophecy and the American Voice (2006)

When That Rough God Goes Riding: Listening to Van Morrison (2010)

Bob Dylan by Greil Marcus, Writings 1968–2010 (2010)

The Doors: A Lifetime of Listening to Five Mean Years (2011)

AS EDITOR

Stranded (1979, 2007)

Psychotic Reactions & Carburetor Dung by Lester Bangs (1987)

The Rose & the Briar: Death, Love and Liberty in the American Ballad (2004, with Sean Wilentz)

Best Music Writing 2009 (2009)

A New Literary History of America (2009, with Werner Sollors)

The History of Rock 'n' Roll in Ten Songs

GREIL MARCUS

Yale
UNIVERSITY PRESS
New Haven & London

To everyone I left out

Contents

Most of the recordings, live performances, and movie scenes
mentioned in these pages can be found on YouTube.

But the life one leads cuts out all the lives one might have led; one is never a virgin twice; events engrave themselves. Life is a unity to the soul. We meet events halfway; they are part of us, and we are part of them; and nothing is incidental. Ahead comes the point where all events exist at once, and no new ones are in sight, the point on the edge of death, which is a reckoning point. It is the motion towards this that one tries to halt by crying, "Do you love me? Respect me? Will you always remember me?"

—MALCOLM BRADBURY, *Eating People Is Wrong*, 1959

The History of Rock 'n' Roll in Ten Songs

A New Language

llen Ruppersberg is a Los Angeles artist best known for his 1969 *Al's Café*, a restaurant where the functioning menu featured dishes composed entirely of locally scavenged objects, plates included, and for his 2003 transformation of Allen Ginsberg's "Howl" into a series of so-called singing posters. "A few years ago, on a trip back to Cleveland, I went to the Rock and Roll Hall of Fame for the first time," he wrote in 2012. "I found it fun enough, lots of memorabilia, film clips, old records, of course, and the now familiar story of R'n'R, told again in the basically familiar way."

That basically familiar way can be summed up by scrolling through the inductees to the Rock and Roll Hall of Fame, letting the names compose the history of the music, from the first class—the performers Chuck Berry, James Brown, Ray Charles, Sam Cooke, Fats Domino, the Everly Brothers, Buddy Holly, Jerry Lee Lewis, Little Richard, and Elvis Presley; as "non-performers" the 1950s disc jockey Alan Freed, the Sun Records producer Sam Phillips, and the record man John Hammond of Columbia; and as "early influences" the 1930s Mississippi blues singer Robert Johnson, the "Father of Country Music" Jimmie Rodgers, and the boogie woogie pianist Jimmy Yancey—on through the jazz pianist Jelly Roll Morton, the blues singers Ma Rainey and Bessie Smith, the jazz trumpeter Louis Armstrong, the gospel group the Soul Stirrers, the country singer Hank Williams, the folk singers Lead Belly, Woody Guthrie, and Pete Seeger, the nightclub vocal group the Ink Spots, the jazz singer Billie Holiday, the jump-blues bandleader Louis Jordan, the jazz guitarist Charlie Christian, the Los Angeles rhythm and blues bandleader and impresario Johnny Otis, the Western Swing band Bob Wills and His Texas Playboys, the R&B singers Dinah Washington and Charles Brown, the founding rock 'n' roll vocal group the Orioles, the gospel singer Mahalia Jackson, the bluegrass bandleader Bill Monroe, the Texas blues guitarist T-Bone Walker, the jazz singer Nat "King" Cole, the record man Leonard Chess of Chess, the blues singer Muddy Waters, the harmonica player Little Walter, the songwriter Willie Dixon, the blues singer Howlin' Wolf, the New Orleans record man Cosimo Matassa, the guitarist Les Paul, the guitar maker Leo Fender, John Lee Hooker, the blues singer Elmore James, Big Joe Turner, Clyde McPhatter and the Drifters, Bill Haley and the Comets, the songwriter Jesse Stone, the record men Ahmet and Nesuhi Ertegun, Paul Ackerman, Jerry Wexler, and Tom Dowd of Atlantic, Bo Diddley, the record man Milt Gabler of Decca, the New Orleans pianist Professor Longhair, the pianist Johnnie Johnson, the guitarist Scotty Moore, the

bassist Bill Black, the drummer D. J. Fontana, the songwriter Otis Blackwell, the record man Syd Nathan of King,
Jackie Wilson, the Platters, the New Orleans songwriter and
bandleader Dave Bartholomew, the Coasters, the songwriters Jerry Leiber and Mike Stoller, the saxophonist King Cur-
tis, Carl Perkins, LaVern Baker, Lloyd Price, the record man
Art Rupe of Specialty, Roy Orbison, Ruth Brown, Gene
Vincent and the Blue Caps, the rockabilly singer Wanda
Jackson, Johnny Cash, Ricky Nelson, the guitarist and
producer Chet Atkins, the guitarist James Burton, Jimmy
Reed, the record man Ralph Bass, Little Willie John, the
Moonglows, the Flamingos, Frankie Lymon and the Teen-
agers, the Dells, Eddie Cochran, Little Anthony and the
Imperials, Dion, Hank Ballard, Bobby Darin, the promoter
Dick Clark, the songwriter Doc Pomus, Ritchie Valens, the
Impressions, Brenda Lee, the New Orleans songwriter and
producer Allen Toussaint, the pianist Floyd Cramer, the
New Orleans drummer Earl Palmer, the guitarist Freddie
King, the Famous Flames, the Miracles, the record man
Berry Gordy, Jr., of Motown, Bobby "Blue" Bland, the
Isley Brothers, Duane Eddy, Etta James, Miles Davis, the
producer Phil Spector, Gene Pitney, Darlene Love, the
Ronettes, the drummer Hal Blaine, the songwriter Mort
Shuman, the Ventures, the Shirelles, the Beach Boys, Buddy
Guy, Del Shannon, the Aldon Music songwriters Carole
King and Gerry Goffin, Ellie Greenwich and Jeff Barry, and

Barry Mann and Cynthia Weil, the Aldon Music publisher Don Kirshner, Marvin Gaye, Bob Dylan, the Temptations, the Four Seasons, the Four Tops, the producers and song-writers Brian Holland, Lamont Dozier, and Eddie Holland of Motown, Stevie Wonder, Martha and the Vandellas, Sol-omon Burke, Ike and Tina Turner, the Beatles, the Beatles manager Brian Epstein, the producer George Martin, the Rolling Stones, the Rolling Stones manager Andrew Loog Oldham, the Dave Clark Five, the Righteous Brothers, the Supremes, the bassist James Jamerson and the drummer Benny Benjamin of Motown's Funk Brothers, the Lovin' Spoonful, Dusty Springfield, the Byrds, the Who, the Hol-lies, the record man Lou Adler of Dunhill, Otis Redding, Sam and Dave, Booker T. and the M.G.'s, the record man Jim Stewart of Stax-Volt, the Kinks, the Young Rascals, Van Morrison, Simon and Garfunkel, the Animals, Donovan, the Yardbirds, Jefferson Airplane, the Grateful Dead, Janis Joplin, the concert promoter Bill Graham, Aretha Franklin, B. B. King, the Doors, the record man Jac Holzman of Elek-tra, the Velvet Underground, Wilson Pickett, Percy Sledge, Bobby Womack, the record man Clive Davis of Columbia and Arista, Neil Diamond, Smokey Robinson, Albert King, Frank Zappa, Buffalo Springfield, Cream, Sly and the Fam-ily Stone, Curtis Mayfield, the Staple Singers, the Mamas and the Papas, the Jimi Hendrix Experience, Pink Floyd, the Small Faces, Creedence Clearwater Revival, Leonard

Cohen, Fleetwood Mac, the Bee Gees, Dr. John, Santana, Jann Wenner of *Rolling Stone*, the Band, Neil Young, the San Francisco disc jockey Tom Donahue, Alice Cooper, Isaac Hayes, Crosby, Stills and Nash, the Jackson 5, Traffic, the producer Glyn Johns, the O'Jays, the producers Kenny Gamble and Leon Huff, Randy Newman, Rod Stewart, Jeff Beck, Cat Stevens, Led Zeppelin, the Stooges, John Lennon, Paul McCartney, George Harrison, the Eagles, Elton John, Paul Simon, the record man Mo Ostin of Warner Bros., Linda Ronstadt, the saxophonist Steve Douglas, Bob Seger, Jimmy Cliff, Al Green, the self-proclaimed Master of Time and Space Leon Russell, Gladys Knight and the Pips, Bob Marley, the record man Chris Blackwell of Island, ABBA, Eric Clapton, the Allman Brothers Band, the organist Spooner Oldham, Joni Mitchell, Jackson Browne, Laura Nyro, the record man David Geffen of Asylum and Geffen, David Bowie, Parliament/Funkadelic, Billy Joel, Lynyrd Skynyrd, Genesis, the record men Herb Alpert and Jerry Moss of A&M, Bruce Springsteen and the E Street Band, Earth, Wind and Fire, Bonnie Raitt, James Taylor, Black Sabbath, Michael Jackson, the producer Quincy Jones, Steely Dan, Queen, Kiss, Aerosmith, Heart, Donna Summer, the Ramones, Patti Smith, Blondie, the Sex Pistols (who declined), Talking Heads, Tom Petty and the Heartbreakers, the Clash, the Police, Elvis Costello and the Attractions, Rush, Hall and Oates, AC/DC, ZZ Top, Prince,

Madonna, the Pretenders, U2, the record man Seymour Stein of Sire, the concert promoter Frank Barsalona, R.E.M., Van Halen, Grandmaster Flash and the Furious Five, John Mellencamp, Run-D.M.C., Tom Waits, Public Enemy, Metallica, the Beastie Boys, Peter Gabriel, Guns N' Roses, the Red Hot Chili Peppers, Nirvana, and, likely over the next years, at some point past the eligibility date of twenty-five years after their first recording, N.W.A, Tupac Shakur, Pearl Jam, Radiohead, Green Day, the Notorious B.I.G., Lil Wayne, the Roots, Eminem, Beyoncé, and Jay-Z.

Born in 1944, Allen Ruppersberg is by nature a collector, or a canvasser, someone who maps a territory by picking his way through it like a magpie. Possessed by the sense that "in some cases, if you live long enough, you begin to see the endings of the things in which you saw the beginnings," he left the Rock and Roll Hall of Fame and, starting with the discovery of a one-dollar ten-inch Little Richard 78, circled through his native Ohio in a pursuit of the origins of the music, in thrift shops, church sales, library sell-offs, estate sales, and eviction auctions, ultimately amassing, along with boxes of sheet music, music magazines, music-themed family photographs, and fan club photos, more than four thousand 78s and 45s, beginning with so-called coon songs and minstrelsy, then moving through the musical country first mapped by Harry Smith's 1952 eighty-four-song anthology of 1920s and '30s 78s he originally gave the plain, definitive title *American Folk Music*, through country, blues, gospel, and finally rock 'n' roll as it announced and defined itself and, to Ruppersberg, reached its end, from Vess L. Ossman's 1906 "Darkies' Awakening" to Al Green's 1975 "Could I Be the One?" "Listening to these records," he wrote, "the history that seemed so familiar in the Rock and Roll Hall of Fame became again unfamiliar and a much richer and more original understanding was made possible."

A key to a richer and more original understanding—or a different story from the one any conventional, chronological, heroic history of rock 'n' roll seems to tell, from Nik Cohn's *Pop from the Beginning* in 1969 to *The Rolling Stone Illustrated History of Rock & Roll* in 1976 and on down through countless books since then, the most notable likely Cohn's *Rock Dreams* collaboration with the artist Guy Peellaert in 1982—might be to feel one's way through the music as a field of expression, and as a web of affinities. Going back to the Orioles' "It's Too Soon to Know" in 1948 and forward to Lady Gaga's "Bad Romance" sixty-one years later and on from there to the present day, rock 'n' roll may be more than anything a continuum of associations, a drama of direct and spectral connections between songs and performers. It may be a story about the way a song will continue speaking in a radically different setting than the one that, it may have seemed, gave rise to it, a story in which someone may own the copyright but the voice of the song is under no one's control. Rock 'n' roll may be most of all a language that, it declares, can say anything: divine all truths, reveal all mysteries, and escape all restrictions. That was true from the first—which is to say that on the terms rock 'n' roll has set for itself, positing a free-floating Möbius strip of signs, the present day may be an illusion.

As a seemingly newly discovered form of speech, rock 'n' roll proclaimed its novelty in the way in which it became instantly self-referential, a world that, even as it was being built, was complete in itself, a Tower of Babel where whatever was said, however unlikely, no matter how close it was to speaking in tongues, regardless of whether it was babble and meant to be, was instantly understood. "Yahweh came down to watch the city and tower the sons of man were bound to build. 'They are one people, with the same tongue,' said Yahweh. 'They conceive this between them, and it leads up until no boundary exists to what they will touch. Between us, let's descend, baffle their tongue until each is scatterbrain to his friend.'" It didn't work, even if Debbie Reynolds's "Tammy," a treacly movie hit so inescapable in 1957 it swallowed everything else on the radio, made it seem as if rock 'n' roll was a trick its fans had played on themselves, made it seem as if it had never existed at all. That's why the only history of rock 'n' roll that works the way the music talks is Colin B. Morton and Chuck Death's 1980s–1990s comic strip *Great Pop Things*—where, among other manifestations of rock 'n' roll as one infinite and inter-locking pun, as Bob Dylan takes the stage in Manchester, England, in 1966 and, with the Hawks behind him, against a chorus of catcalls from the crowd, storms through likely the most powerful music of his life and is about to launch into his last number, an outraged fan shouts not "Judas!" but, rather, "BOO! Do you know any Judas Priest?"

Whole intellectual industries are devoted to proving that there is nothing new under the sun, that everything comes from something else—and to such a degree that one can never tell when one thing turns into something else. But it is the moment when something appears as if out of nowhere, when a work of art carries within itself the thrill of inven-tion, of discovery, that is worth listening for. It's that moment when a song or a performance is its own manifesto, issuing its own demands on life in its own, new language—which, though the charge of novelty is its essence, is immediately grasped by any number of people who will swear they never heard anything like it before—that speaks. In rock 'n' roll, this is a moment that, in historical time, is repeated again and again, until, as culture, it defines the art itself.

"It's like saying, 'Get all the pop music, put it into a car-tridge, put the cap on it and fire the gun,'" Pete Townshend of the Who said in 1968. "Whether those ten or 15 numbers sound roughly the same. You don't care what period they were written in, what they're all about. It's the bloody explosion that they create when you let the gun off. It's the event. That's what rock and roll is." Any pop record made at any time can contain Pete Townshend's argument. Any such record, from "Breathless" by Jerry Lee Lewis to "Breathless" by the Corrs, will make that argument—which is to say that this book could have comprised solely records issued by the Sun label in Memphis in the 1950s, only records made by female punk bands in the 1990s, or nothing but soul records made in Detroit, Memphis, New York City, San Antonio, New Orleans, Los Angeles, or Chicago in 1963.

From that perspective, there is no reason to be responsible to chronology, to account for all the innovators, to follow the supposed progression of the form. The Maytals' "Funky Kingston" is not a step forward from the Drifters' "Money Honey," or OutKast's "Hey Ya" a step forward from "Funky Kingston." They are rediscoveries of a certain spirit, a leap into style, a step out of time. One can dive into a vault as filled with songs as Uncle Scrooge's was filled with money and come out with a few prizes that at once raise the question of what rock 'n' roll is and answer it.

Who, as the music took shape and developed a memory, was really speaking to whom? What if the real, living connection is not between, say, the Beatles and the Rolling Stones, but between the Beatles and Buddy Holly—or simply, which is to say not simply at all, between a single Buddy Holly song and the Beatles' attempts, across the entire length of their life as a group, to play it? What if Bob Dylan's "It's Alright, Ma (I'm Only Bleeding)" finds its best audience not in any of the crowds that from 1964 to the present have cheered for the line "Even the president of the United States sometimes must have to stand naked" but with A.J. and his new friend sitting in his SUV in the last episode of *The Sopranos*? There they are, kids just out of rehab, parked in the woods with the motor running, A.J. stiff and nervous behind the wheel, the much hipper Rhiannon calm and smoking in the passenger seat. They listen in silence as Dylan's unstoppable rant against every manifestation of modern life reaches such a pitch that "All is phony," the three words sealing a verse, feels like a throwaway. "I know you said this guy was good," A.J. says, as he hears "Meantime life outside goes on all around you." You can't tell if he's truly shocked or if he's trying to seem cool. "It's amazing it was written so long ago," Rhiannon says, as if she's talking about someone who lived before the Civil War. "It's like about right now." As the camera shows smoke from leaves catching fire beneath the SUV coming through the vents, Rhiannon climbs on top of A.J. and begins to pull off her top. Flames rise up under the dashboard. A.J. and Rhiannon tumble out and run. Just before the vehicle explodes, we hear the CD melting, the words and music slowing down into an ugly, indecipherable smear, the song not floating off into the ether but sinking into the slime it was made to describe, until the next person, never having heard of Bob Dylan, stumbles across it.

The official, standard history of rock 'n' roll is true, but it's not the whole truth. It's not the truth at all. It's a constructed story that has been disseminated so comprehensively that people believe it, but it's not true to their experience, and it may even deform or suppress their experience. "I think we all have this little theater on top of our shoulders, where the past and the present and our aspirations and our memories are simply and inexorably mixed," the late Dennis Potter, the creator of sometimes deliriously life-affirming television and movie musicals—*Pennies from Heaven, The Singing Detective, Lipstick on Your Collar*—said in 1987. But what if your memories are not your own, but are, rather, kidnapped by another story, colonized by a larger cultural memory? "It gets dark, you know, very late in Boise, Idaho, in the summer," David Lynch once said of 9 September 1956, when Elvis Presley first appeared on the *Ed Sullivan Show*—a show supposedly watched by 82.6 percent of all Americans watching TV that night. Lynch was ten. "It was not quite dark, so it must have been, like, maybe nine o'clock at night, I'm not sure. That nice twilight, a beautiful night. Deep shadows were occurring. And it was sort of warm. And Willard Burns came running towards me from about three houses down the street, and he said, 'You missed it!' and I said, 'What?' and he said, 'Elvis on *Ed Sullivan!*' And it just, like, set a fire in my head. How could I have missed that? And this was the night, you know. But I'm kind of glad I didn't see it; it was a bigger event in my head because I missed it." "What makes each one of us unique," Dennis Potter went on, talking about his little theater of past and present, aspirations and memories, "is the potency of the individual mix"—and in the history of rock 'n' roll as I hope to trace it, the likes of Lynch's story might count for more than whatever happened on TV that night. Records that made no apparent history other than their own, the faint marks they left on the charts or someone's memory, might count for more than any master narrative that excludes them.

This came into focus for me one day in December 2012, in a diner on Mulberry Street in New York called Parm. They play oldies, some obvious, some not. This day there was Bill Haley and the Comets' 1954 version of Big Joe Turner's "Shake, Rattle and Roll," the Beach Boys' 1966 "Wouldn't It Be Nice," Maurice Williams and the Zodiacs' 1960 "Stay," a version of "Dream Lover" that seemed just slightly off until I realized it wasn't Bobby Darin but Dion, in a 1961 recording I didn't know existed, a speeded-up remix of Sam Cooke's 1960 "Wonderful World" with gruesome strings, Marvin Gaye's 1968 "I Heard It Through the Grapevine," the Chiffons' 1963 "One Fine Day," and Little Richard's 1956 "Long Tall Sally" (I remembered W. T. Lhamon, Jr., writing that while "most audiences probably did not suspect" that Little

Richard's songs were full of gays, transvestites, adulterers, and prostitutes, not to mention adulterous gay transvestite prostitutes, the charge in the music came partly because "the singer knew," the producer Bumps "Blackwell knew, and so did the musicians in Cosimo Matassas's J & M Studio, where they were recording").

In this rich assemblage—random, programmed, which would be more satisfying?—"Stay" stood out. Maurice Williams and the Zodiacs were a South Carolina doo-wop group that formed in 1956 as the Royal Charms. In 1957, as the Gladiolas, they recorded "Little Darlin'" (a song the Canadian glee-club combo the Diamonds, whose EPs included the likes of "On, Wisconsin!" found so cretinous they redid it as a parody of rock 'n' roll, only to see it top the charts as the real thing). The Gladiolas became the Zodiacs in 1957—and compared with what they had done before, "Stay," recorded in 1959 in South Carolina, issued in 1960 in New York, was a cataclysm. A number 1 hit barely a minute and a half long—and a sketch for Wilson Pickett's "In the Midnight Hour" five years later—so much was happening on the record it seemed much longer. Note by note, measure by measure—with Williams's laconic come-on-baby not climbing but suddenly surging to the mad falsetto that, playing off the group's chanted "*STAY! STAY!*" reached the impossible high note in "Sayyyyyyyyyy/You *will*" that had people all over the world, like Tim McIntire's Alan Freed in

Floyd Mutrux's 1978 film *American Hot Wax*, twisting their faces around that last note in joy and wonder until they swallowed it—the record seemed to turn the radio upside down. It was the invention in the music that was so striking —the will to create what had never been heard before, through vocal tricks, rhythmic shifts, pieces of sound that didn't logically follow one from the other, that didn't make musical or even emotional sense when looked at as pieces, but as a whole spoke a new language.

The music—and the market, the audience that it at once revealed and created—was a challenge to whoever had the nerve to try to make it. The ear of the new audience was fickle, teenagers knowing nothing of where the music came from and caring less, and why should they care? It was new, it was different, and that was what they wanted: out of a nascent sense that the world in which their parents had come of age had changed or in some deeper, inexpressible manner disappeared, a sound that made the notion of a new life a fact, even if that fact lasted only a minute and a half. To make that fact—to catch that ear, to sell your record, to top the charts, if only in your dreams—you had to try something new. You had to find something new. You had to listen to everything on the market and try to understand what wasn't there—and what wasn't there was you. So you asked yourself, as people have been asking themselves ever since, what's different about me? How am I different from everybody else—and why am I different? Yes, you invent yourself to the point of stupidity, you give yourself a ridiculous new name, you appear in public in absurd clothes, you sing songs based on nursery rhymes or jokes or catchphrases or advertising slogans, and you do it for money, renown, to lift yourself up, to escape the life you were born to, to escape the poverty, the racism, the killing strictures of a life that you were raised to accept as fate, to make yourself a new person not only in the eyes of the world, but finally in your own eyes too. A minute and a half, two minutes, maybe three, in the one-time, one-take fantasy that takes place in the recording studio, whatever it might be—for "Stay," a Quonset hut—or forever, even a year, even a few months, in the heaven of the charts, where one more hit means the game isn't over, that you don't have to go back to the prison of fate, that you can once again experience the satisfaction that only art, only the act of putting something new into the world, can bring.

No one would have thought of it that way, one might say—not Maurice Williams or for that matter any of the Zodiacs, not the Beach Boys, Little Richard, Sam Cooke, Elvis Presley, Robert Johnson, Jimmie Rodgers, or Dion covering Bobby Darin to fill out his *Runaround Sue* LP. One might say that, and one might be wrong.

In 2012 the record collectors Richard Nevins, Pete Whelan, and Dick Spottswood were sitting on Spottswood's porch in Florida, talking about Mississippi blues singers recording in the late 1920s and early 1930s, sometimes for ten dollars or a few shots of whiskey a song, singers who reappeared in the 1960s, found like records by collectors and brought north to appear at folk festivals and make the twelve-song album that in their time did not exist. They were arguing with the "cold dispassionate" blues scholars who said musicians "played the blues for money, they didn't play for any other reason," and "the over-romanticizing" musical historians who claimed "that the blues were a cathartic release of all this social pain." "Black folks played music for the same reason white people did," Nevins said. "They wanted money, they wanted women, they wanted to express themselves and be respected and they didn't want to be out plowing 4 acres of cotton."

"Well," said Spottswood, "I would hope artistry becomes an end in itself. I know conversations I would have with Skip James, Robert Wilkins and John Hurt would be about the excellence of the music and what made the music good. And how they tried to be as good as they wanted to be, because being good was better than being bad. One thing that old blues records teach you, is that even people with very limited skills can play very personal, distinctive, and appealing music that has nothing to do with the extent of their technique. It was their artistry. It was their feeling."

Shake Some Action

1976

The only thing that rock & roll did *not* get from country and blues was a sense of consequences," the writer Bill Flanagan said to Neil Young in 1986. "In country and blues, if you raised hell on Saturday night, you were gonna feel real bad on Sunday morning when you dragged yourself to church. Or when you didn't drag yourself to church." "That's right," Young said. "Rock & roll is reckless abandon. Rock & roll is the *cause* of country and blues. Country and blues came first, but somehow rock & roll's place in the course of events is dispersed"—and what a remarkable thing to say that is. "There's a fish in my stomach a thousand years old," Brett Sparks of the Handsome Family sang slowly, over a heavy, lumbering fuzztone in "Winnebago Skeletons" ten years after Young spoke—not likely meant as an image for rock 'n' roll as a force, a spirit, a joke, that was there all along, like that fish waiting for the chance to get out, but it speaks the language.

You can hear Young's epistemology come to life in a thousand records, from Fats Domino's "The Fat Man" in 1950 to Young's own "Surfer Joe and Moe the Sleaze" to a group without a name yet stumbling on the right, preordained, never-known way to get from one place to another in their version of "Smells Like Teen Spirit," which Kurt Cobain was once happy to admit was Nirvana's version of "Louie Louie," the all-time number 1 garage-band hit—a song lost by its composer, Richard Berry, in the throat-cutting small-label competition that ruled rock 'n' roll in Los Angeles in 1956, and found, for good, when Rockin' Robin Roberts picked it out of a bin in Tacoma in 1958. He recorded his own version in 1961. Two years later he watched, along with Richard Berry, as the Kingsmen and Paul Revere and the Raiders, who cut their versions in the same Portland studio one day apart, made it not only the most popular but, it was somehow clear, the most archetypal song in the country— the Raiders taking the Pacific Coast, the Kingsmen the rest of the nation—as if it had always been there. But I never hear Young's words translated with more urgency, with more joy, than in the Flamin' Groovies' "Shake Some Action." "I really try to do something every time I go out there that stretches my capabilities, that puts *me* on the edge of going too far," Young said one October day on Skyline Boulevard, thirty miles down from San Francisco, in 1993. "Where it might not work. Where the song may be too new, may not be the right song—but if I deliver the song right, and I'm really into the song, then it'll make people forget who I am." You can hear that all through Young's career, in the successively more impossible guitar passages in "Cowgirl in the Sand," in "Over and Over," in the music he improvised for

Jim Jarmusch's film *Dead Man*, and you can hear it too in "Shake Some Action"—but with the certain feeling, in the song that was there all along, that for as long as it lasts the music has called up the players, not the other way around.

The Flamin' Groovies—a name so stupid it can't transcend its own irony, a name so stupid it's embarrassing to say out loud ("Where're you going tonight?" "I'm going to see the, the—you know, that San Francisco band Roy Loney used to have before he left")—made more than a dozen albums, and one song, recorded in 1972, unheard until 1976. They began in 1965 as the Chosen Few; by 1976, with Chris Wilson at the microphone, the band was still playing bars. Cyril Jordan was still playing guitar and writing the songs. "It was the only free country left in the world," he once said, not talking about America but about rock 'n' roll in America, or anywhere else. "No boundaries, no passports. There wasn't even a government." By 1976, rock 'n' roll might have seemed like an old story, fixed and static, its secrets all exposed, a fact to learn: precisely a government, run by a few record companies and half a dozen lifeless icons. But in "Shake Some Action" everything is new, as if the secret had been discovered and the mystery solved on the spot. No founding rock 'n' roll statement—Howlin' Wolf's "How Many More Years," the Drifters' "Let the Boogie Woogie Roll," Little Richard's "Tutti Frutti" or "Ready Teddy," Jerry Lee Lewis's "Whole Lotta Shakin' Goin' On" or "Lovin' Up a Storm," the Chantels' "If You Try," Elvis Presley's "Jail-house Rock," Dion and the Belmonts' "I Wonder Why"—creates the same moment more fully, but that is not really the point. The point is that before rock 'n' roll, as it was defined by those performers, those records, and a thousand more, nothing like what happens in "Shake Some Action" had ever been heard on earth; the point is that rock 'n' roll, as music, as an argument about life captured in sound, as a beat, was something new under the sun, and it was new here, in 1976, in the hands of a few people in San Francisco. In that sense, more than twenty years after that fact first emerged to be learned, "Shake Some Action" can itself serve as a founding statement. "OLYMPIA, the birthplace of rock," you could have read on the back of an album issued by the Kill Rock Stars label of Olympia, Washington, in 1991. That meant rock 'n' roll could be invented anywhere, at any time, regardless of any rumors that something vaguely similar might have happened before.

The story told in "Shake Some Action" is complete in its title—though in the song it's a wish, not a fact, a desperate wish the singer doesn't expect to come true. The words hardly matter: "Need" "Speed" "Say" "Away" are enough. It starts fast, as if in the middle of some greater song. A bright, trebly guitar counts off a theme, a beat is set, a bass note seems to explode, sending a shower of light over all the notes around it. The rhythm is pushing, but somehow it's falling behind the singer. He slows down to let it catch up, and then the sound the guitar is making, a bell chiming through the day, has shot past both sides. Every beat is pulling back against every other; the whole song is a backbeat, every swing a backhand, every player his own free country, discovering the real free country in the song as it rises up in front of him, glimpsing that golden land, losing it as the mirage fades, blinking his eyes, getting it back, losing it again—that is its reckless abandon, the willingness of the music, in pursuit of where it needs to go, where it must go, to abandon itself. "You have to go into a crowd and do something they can't," Young said that day in 1993. "Some of them are hearing it and some of them aren't, but it doesn't matter. The idea is the *tension*."

In "Shake Some Action," the tension is there from the first moments—that count is a count to the end, the dead end, the door you've locked from the inside and can't open, and the whole song can feel like an attempt to escape the tension, to let it dissipate, until the musicians no longer remember that the theme that kicked them off was fate. Here, every element in the music is a leap. As different parts of the song slow, as others pick up speed, depending on where you are, which wave in the song you're riding, the sense of imminent loss can disappear—and then the singer drops back and there is a guitar, more than a guitarist, replacing the story you've heard with one you haven't.

It's what the singer is afraid of losing defined now purely in the positive, as flight, as freedom, in Norman Mailer's words loose in the water for the first time in your life, because no matter how many times in how many pieces of music you are swept away as the instrumental passages in "Shake Some Action" can sweep you away, it's always the first time. When the guitarist steps onto the magic carpet of his first solo, it is a picture of everything the singer is certain is slipping away from him, but it is not slipping away, it is present, you can hold it in your hand, see it glow. At the end, the guitarist again steps forward—and while the notes played might on paper be the same as they were before, in the air they are speaking in a different tongue. The drum roll that has tripped the song into the instrumental passage that will end it has tripped it over a cliff, and you feel not the worth of what the singer wants, but what it was worth, before it vanished, before it went back beyond memory, into fantasy, as if desire never had a face. Is that why you have to play the song again, to make it come out differently? Or because you can't live without that beat?

Transmission

2007·1979·2010

In Anton Corbijn's 2007 film *Control*, it's 20 September 1978, in Manchester, England: the local television show *Granada Reports* is about to present a new band. "Seeing as how this is the first television program which brought you the first appearances from everyone from the Beatles to the Buzzcocks, we like to think we bring you the most new and interesting sounds in the North West. They're called Joy Division, and are a Manchester band except for the guitarist, who comes from Salford, a very important distinction," says the Granada host Tony Wilson, played pallidly by Craig Parkinson, speaking quietly in a monotone broken only by a condescendingly ironic twist on *very*. "This—is called 'Transmission.'" As the camera pulls back, we see a fancy, corny set, with each musician—the singer Ian Curtis, the guitarist Bernard Sumner, and the bassist Peter Hook, born in 1956, and the drummer Stephen Morris, born in 1957—isolated on his own round riser. Wilson steps off the riser he's been sharing with Curtis, standing much too close to him.

The odd thing about this conventionally flat introduction, which despite the fact that it lasts only twenty seconds is almost unbearable, is that, throughout, Sam Riley, playing Ian Curtis, who would hang himself twenty months after the actual Granada broadcast, is standing behind Wilson

31

with his head bowed. He doesn't move. You can imagine that he's praying, for some dark night of his soul or just that Wilson will finish and get off the go-go dancer platform and leave him alone. You can imagine you're watching more than that: someone suddenly paralyzed by doubt, self-loathing, or a wish to disappear.

Led by a thick, ground-up bass shudder—the guitarist's *ba-DING ba-DING* of the first Manchester punk single, the Buzzcocks' "Boredom" from late 1976, now a harsher, threatening sound, the bassist's sound of a train coming to a stop in the middle of nowhere, *ba-DAH ba-DAH*—the band breaks into a slow, up-and-down drone, its own kind of monotone. Curtis—Riley—sways back and forth behind the microphone stand. His eyes flash on whatever is before him in the studio, then close; they seem to fall closed. The camera shifts to Stephen Morris, played by Harry Tread-away, Peter Hook, played by Joe Anderson, Bernard Sumner, played by James Anthony Pearson, Morris concentrating hard, Hook looking serious and altogether at home, Sumner careful. On the soundtrack, the actors are playing their own instruments and Riley is doing his own singing, but there's no sense of that. The actors have disappeared into the gravity of the song as it begins, each modulation in tone seeming like a promise that the rhythm will move forward, a promise that is immediately taken back.

After a little more than half a minute, Riley—Curtis—

begins to sing. "Radio," he almost barks in his own mono-tone. "Live transmission," he croons, the words spinning. His voice is deeper than you expect from his slight frame, or the home-cut of his Roman bangs. He looks as if the words are hard to get out, as if they weigh too much—that these three bare words carry too much social or aesthetic mean-ing, or that they are too burdensome simply as verbal ob-jects, as phonetic facts you must form in your mouth, facts the singer might prefer to deny, but can't. Elvis Costello's "Radio Radio," a raging, superbly constructed pop song with a punk heart, would be on the radio that same year, damn-ing everything about the medium from the giant transmitter in London to the little box in the singer's bed-sit as instru-ments of a zombie culture that will lead to the extinction of all human emotion everywhere on earth—"I want to bite the hand that feeds me," the pop singer says, and you believe him—but what is coming out of Curtis is on another plane, closer to a dream, or insomnia. Regardless of the unstop-pable ride Costello gave his argument, at bottom he defined a political problem. "Transmission" is not an argument. It's a dramatization of the realization that the act of listening to the radio is a suicidal gesture. It will kill your mind. It will rob your soul.

Curtis—Riley—raises his left arm, points a finger in the air, singing now about the primacy of silence, because it's superior to anything that might be on the radio, or because in the world the song is making, the radio has lost the capacity to broadcast anything else. Even as Riley—Curtis—follows the slides in the rhythm, catches the dying fall at the end of each passage, the drumming increases in force, in an affirmation that you're going to be listening to a story you might not want to hear. Riley comes off of that, too. The words get heavier. As if to lift them, or strengthen his body against what it's being forced to carry, Curtis, dressed in well-pressed trousers and a long-sleeved shirt, the clothes loose but determinedly respectable, begins to pump his arms. Then again he lifts one arm and points, and then begins a chant.

Though the music made by the band gains in precision, takes on muscle and shape, finds a quality of insistence that makes it seem as if the tempo has increased even though it hasn't, the music also continues as it has; there is an increase in pressure inside the body the song has inhabited from the first. For Curtis everything has changed. What was, no matter how convincing the little drama of weight and obligation, simply a song, a number, a TV appearance, is now a cauldron, and in that cauldron all songs, the band's songs, every song they've ever heard, every song that has ever been played, the impulse to make sound, the desire to sing and play itself, is boiling over. Curtis is boiling over. Riley is boiling over—or he is simply playing someone who's boiling over, but that's hard to credit as you watch. Curtis's arms begin to windmill in tight circles. His shoulders jump. He's a marionette who has just discovered that his movements are not his but can't remember a puppetmaster; he's a man turning a large piece of machinery with arms that don't belong to him. His eyes dart over here, over there, bulging with horror at what he's seeing, what he's seeing far beyond the studio, outside its walls, maybe in the streets as they were when the four walked into the studio and as they'll be when they leave, maybe in the past, maybe in the future; he doesn't want to be here but he has no choice. He is almost screaming now, his face breaking up, his words weirdly holding their shape, perfectly clear in the absolute panic that, musically, is putting the words across—"Language is sound, that's all we need know"—the panic that on the level beneath the plane of musical communication has rendered his words, any words, irrelevant, a bad joke, a lie. His arms jerk, but with such intensity they carry their own grace: you can't take your eyes off them, you don't want the movements to stop. The music breaks, slows down, comes to a halt as if the music is physically coming apart, instrument by instrument, piece by piece, idea by idea. Sitting in the theater, watching the movie, I realized that half a minute had passed and I hadn't taken a breath.

In real time, with people walking into a room to hear the band play, the same thing happened throughout 1978 and 1979, in London, Paris, Amsterdam, in Manchester time and again. Watching Corbijn's movie now, you can notice, near the end of the song, a shot of the actor playing Peter Hook leaning into a microphone, adding a backing vocal to Curtis's "Dance, dance, dance—to the radio"—which as a line in a song is precisely what the Beach Boys were doing in the car in "Dance, Dance, Dance" in 1964, but something else as a line from Jeremiah, which is how Curtis is delivering it, or how the line is delivering him—and be stopped cold. What? Another band member putting in a rehearsed effect to give the performance a little more impact? You mean this was a show?

Over and over again, this is what happened in "Transmission." There would be nights when the song froze, when its gestures lost their language and the rhythm reached a point where it could no longer tell the band anything it hadn't heard before, when the audience demanded to hear it, which told the musicians that the audience knew exactly what to expect, and they could no longer give the audience, even the song, the lie. Then on another night the song would return to claim what it rightfully deserved. As a typically elegant Joy Division song it was the most unstable song they could play.

Like the Buzzcocks, like many other Manchester bands, some never going beyond fantasy, some heard around the world, Joy Division had its genesis in the show the Sex Pistols played in the Lesser Free Trade Hall in Manchester on 4 June 1976. Depending on which story you believe, there were forty people there—some of them, well before the Sex

Pistols had released an actual record, already calling out for favorite numbers—or maybe sixty, even a hundred; no one has ever said there were more than that. It was a fearsome, thrilling show; from an audience tape of that night, it sounds like an initiation into a secret society. Halfway through, with "No Feelings," relentless, the song building on itself with every beat, with every iteration of its idea, you can physically sense how shocking it all must have been. "God, what the fuck is this?" Tony Wilson wrote in 2002, looking back to that night, when by his count he'd been one of forty-two people in the crowd:

> Bloody hell, it's Stepping Stone. And in the next sixty seconds, hearing the Pistols violently murder and then resurrect this simple pop classic, all was made clear as all was destroyed. Only in hearing the old was the new revealed. I will destroy the temple and in three minutes I will rebuild it, sayeth the Lord, sayeth Johnny Rotten. Clarity for the one academic arsehole in the audience. The tune, the song, the lyrics, the beat of this Monkees gem were assailed with utter confidence, utter anger. In its complete indifference to the niceties of technique and respect, they restored to the popular song the spirit that is the only fucking reason it exists in the first place. Robert Johnson sold his soul at the crossroads. He sold it for this. Good deal.

Two of the people there were Peter Hook and Bernard Sumner. "I saw the Sex Pistols," Sumner would say. "They were terrible. I wanted to get up and be terrible, too." They pledged themselves as a band that night; their first name was Stiff Little Kittens. Curtis, who Hook and Sumner had met at a second Manchester Sex Pistols show two weeks later, answered a SINGER WANTED ad they put up at Virgin Records. They changed the name to Warsaw. Running through various drummers until they found Morris, they were an indistinguishable punk band, trying to be frantic, reaching for a screech ("'Yeah yeah yeah yeah fuck off fuck off,'" as Sumner would sum it up), more than that reaching for a no that they themselves could believe, even if they couldn't get anyone else to believe it. In 1978 they found it. "We were doing a soundcheck at the Mayflower, in May," Hook said in 2007, "and we played 'Transmission': people had been moving around, and they all stopped to listen. I was thinking, what's the matter with that lot? That's when I realized that was our first great song." "Now, finally, he understood the straightforward filter in his head," said Tony Wilson, who founded Factory Records for Joy Division and other Manchester bands.

> He had chosen artists who "meant it." More than meant it. Had no choice. The stuff was forcing itself up and out of their psyches whether they fucking liked it or not. 99.99% of bands are on stage 'cause they want to be in the music business, they want to be on *Top of the Pops*, they want to be rock and roll stars. The very few are on stage because

they have absolutely no fucking choice. Whatever is demanding to be expressed pushes them forward. No choice. And that night Warsaw had no choice but to be up there playing this searing music.

"None of us were interested in any kind of achievement, in a success, celebrity form, or money," Peter Hook said in 2013. "It was the drive to play. Just to be heard."

"The unearned euphoria of *Henderson the Rain King*; the shapeless piety of *A Fable*; the sentimental self-indulgence of *Across the River and into the Trees*; the maudlin falsity of *The Town*; the heavy-handed symbolism and religiosity of *The Old Man and the Sea*, destined from its inception for the pages of *Life*—such failures make over and over the point that the contemporary American writer can abjure negativism only if he is willing to sacrifice truth and art," Leslie Fiedler wrote in 1960, in the introduction to *No! In Thunder*.

> For major novelists and minor, the pursuit of the positive means stylistic suicide. Language itself decays, and dialogue becomes travesty; character, stereotype; insight, sentiment. The Nobel Prize speech destined for high-school anthologies requires quite another talent from that demanded by the novel; and the abstract praise of love requires another voice from that which cries *No!* to the most noble temptations, the most defensible lies.
>
> Yet one must not forget, in the face of their recent de-

cline, the success of Bellow and Hemingway and Faulkner: the terrible impact of *The Victim*, *The Sun Also Rises* and *The Sound and the Fury*. The last, in particular, remains the exemplary American novel, perhaps the greatest work of fiction produced in the United States in the twentieth century. And it is no accident that its title comes from the bleakest passage in Shakespeare, or that its action begins inside the mind of an idiot. The point is insisted upon bluntly, almost too obviously: life is a tale told by an idiot, full of sound and fury, signifying nothing. Here is the ultimate negation, the Hard No pressed as far as it will go. Yet "nothing" is not quite Faulkner's last word, only the next to the last. In the end, the negativist is no nihilist, for he affirms the void. Having endured a vision of the meaninglessness of existence, he retreats neither into self-pity nor into a realm of beautiful lies. He chooses, rather, to render the absurdity which he perceives, to know it and make it known. To know and to render, however, means to give it form; and to give form is to provide the possibility of delight—a delight which does not deny horror but lives at its intolerable heart.

Or, *I read Faulkner*—or Sartre, Nietzsche, Hesse, Ballard, Dostoyevsky, as Curtis did. *He said that life was terrible. I wanted to get up and tell people life was terrible, too.* That was the idea of the band. They had named themselves Joy Division after brothels in Nazi concentration camps filled with prisoners. "The oppressed, not the oppressors," Hook insisted. "Quite punk," everyone said: "Great name."

Their first record, a four-song EP called *An Ideal for Living*, featured a drawing of a boy who looked all too much like a member of Hitler Youth banging a drum. Their songs, taking them through Fiedler's labyrinth of self-betrayal and weakness of nerve and coming out the other side, told them how much richer the idea was than such a picture, and how much more dangerous. As Tony Wilson would say of Joy Division when their real songs began to arrive, "Punk was just a single, venomous one-syllable, two-syllable phrase of anger—which was necessary to reignite rock & roll. But sooner or later, someone was going to want to say more than fuck you. Someone was going to want to say, I'm fucked."

Anton Corbijn could have called his film after Joy Division's song "Atmosphere"—shooting in black and white, without dragging his camera over such punk antiurbanism clichés as blocks of rotting council housing or dead-end streets, he pictured Manchester as a place that in giving birth to the Industrial Revolution gave birth as well to an immiserating poverty so ingrained, so close to nature, that it foreclosed all possibilities of vanity or style. As the band members meet in apartments, as Curtis, working for a government employment office to find jobs for disabled people, talks to people who will never have a job, even the rooms seem to have clouds in them. "I found it very difficult to listen to," Sumner said of the first Joy Division album, *Unknown Pleasures*, released in June 1979, except for "She's Lost Control" all of the most memorable songs carrying titles of a single word: "Disorder," "Shadowplay," "Wilderness," "Interzone." It wasn't that it didn't make sense to Sumner, that he wondered where it all came from. That he could explain where it all came from so specifically, to the point of reduction—

> It was because the whole neighborhood that I'd grown up in was completely decimated in the mid-sixties . . . When people say about the darkness in Joy Division's music, by the age of twenty-two I'd had quite a lot of loss in my life. The place where I used to live, where I had my happiest memories, all that had gone. All that was left was a chemical factory. I realized then I could never go back to that happiness. So there's this void. For me Joy Division was about the death of my community and my childhood. It was absolutely irretrievable.

—suggested that there were far more threatening specters in the music. As the critic Jon Savage wrote in a review of the album, "the song titles read an opaque manifesto." There were matters that could be shaped into songs—coherent, interlocking patterns that did affirm form and the possibility of delight—but which were not subject to merely personal, psychological, or sociological explanations. "There is always a social explanation for what we see in art," Albert Camus said in 1947. "Only it doesn't explain anything important." The songs were art, which by definition escapes the control, the intentions, and the technique of the people who make it.

Art doesn't explain itself. "He was Ian, Mister Polite, Mister Nice," Sumner would say, "and then suddenly onstage, about the third song in, you'd notice that he'd gone a bit weird, started pulling the stage apart, ripping up the floorboards and throwing them at the audience. Then by the end of the set he'd be completely covered in blood. But no-one would talk about it, because that was our way; we didn't think he knew why he got himself worked up that way."

At the end of 1978, Curtis had his first epilepsy attack, in a van; his bandmates took him to the hospital. The next April, he began having fits on stage. "Some nights to the end of the set"—some nights lasting only through the end of "Transmission"—"Ian would scatter the mike stand, stagger speedily sideways and be rushed off the stage by Hooky or Barney or Terry their road manager," Tony Wilson would write. "Holding him down was tough. Terry was best at it. 'How are you feeling?' 'What?' 'You OK?' said Rob. The van was quiet. A little aftershocked. 'It's nothing, shut up,' replied Ian curtly."

In January 1980, Curtis made his first suicide attempt, cutting his wrists. In April he tried again, with an overdose of phenobarbitone. On May 18 he succeeded. But that explains nothing about why, in "Transmission" as it was captured on record or on video, the song is not an occasion for explanation, but an event, where what seemed impossible before the event took place seems inevitable afterward. It's no matter that the event, if that is what "Transmission" is, was staged, that it was the integrity of form on the part of the band that allowed Curtis to attack the legitimacy of form, the very idea; no one knew what was going to happen when the song happened. To Deborah Curtis, Curtis's wife, Jon Savage has written, "Ian's mesmeric style mirrored the ever more frequent epileptic spasms that she had to cope with at home"—but the biographical is just another mode of denying the autonomous nature of any work of art, for erasing art as a field where what is at issue, whatever that might be, is not only expressed but discovered. Curtis's performance might have been a mirror of his epilepsy. But it might also have been a matter of intentionally replicating fits, re-enacting them, using them as a form of energy and a form of music, as form as such. More deeply, it might have been a matter of Curtis's using his fits as an idea, the idea for which the songs were only containers. Was it a matter of calling up the demon, and letting it take the stage? Curtis told Sumner how disturbed he was that while once he had struggled to write songs, now they arrived complete, unbidden: "The words were writing themselves."

An attempt to record "Transmission" in March 1979 was vague, muffled; everything sounded contrived. A few months later, the band recorded it again, in a version released as a single, with a lightness in the rhythm, the guitar languid, and, you could imagine, someone who'd wandered into the studio and started carrying on about nothing, until he wanders away. But the song was never about the recording studio. On 13 July 1979 the band played the Factory club in Manchester. For "Dead Souls," Peter Hook's bass playing feels as if it's coming from out of the ground, as if mining is going on beneath the stage. Curtis is inflamed from the start. In "She's Lost Control," part of what is scary is the way the singer maintains control: *he's lying*, the song's second mind says behind its words, its beat, the stitch-by-stitch countdown of what stands in for a melody, *don't believe me*. In "Shadowplay" the singer might have left the hall altogether, singing from the street, accosting people to tell them to beware, to watch out, to look both ways and then step off the curb with their eyes closed. Pressure builds, and by the time the band gets to "Transmission" the crowd is drunk and loud. The music rushes past Curtis, and he makes no attempt to catch up. His singing is abstracted from itself; it's been an extraordinary show, but what's happening here doesn't fit with anything that's come before, and nothing will come after it. Lines in the song begin to fray, pants dragging in the gutter, each unraveling thread a signifier without an object. It is unhinged—you can't imagine what it would have been like to see this, if, in the moment, you would have been capable of seeing what now, in the comfort of your own room, with the singer dead and the rest of the band having gone on for more than thirty years as New Order, you can hear, and conjure up out of your own imagination. "Dance, dance, dance"—the words shatter, the rest of the band shouting behind Curtis. He doesn't need them; they want to be part of it, to testify that they too are alive in this moment. "Dance, dance, dance, to the radio"—as the words batter against each other, nothing could be more loathsome, degrading, immoral.

"I always felt that the 'Dance to the radio' bit was a bit of a cop-out, on that song," Peter Hook said in 2013. "It seemed to be courting the radio, to me." "To get airplay?" I asked. "Yes," he said. "Which is what Tony did say to me once. But when I spoke to Ian about it, it was the opposite. *'It was a call to arms'*—against the radio. It made me reevaluate the whole thing. But *I*—being the *bass player*"—he laughed out loud at himself—"felt that it was the other way around!"

It wasn't that Hook ever missed the black hole of the song. "When you play it," he said, repeating how a friend described it, "you push the whole beat, you're playing in front of the beat, every note, so the rest of them are always trying to catch up with you, and that's what gives it the urgency. From a bass player's point of view, it's a very, very simple riff. It's a repetitious two-note riff, that you can really only—take up and down. In intensity. You can sit back on the verses, you can pound it out on the chorus, but the riff never really changes. The riff is the solid backbone of the song. The song actually changes quite a lot—around the bass riff. The vocals are very, very—almost Neanderthal. When it gets to that, *Dahhhhhnce*"—with a dredging sound coming up behind the word as Hook pulls it out of his throat—"to play, to sing—the looks on people's faces, when you do it, you actually tap in to a basic primal instinct with that roar. That Ian did so wonderfully. People cannot believe—every single piece—even to *hate* you, and be there to watch you fall on your *ass*—they still cannot believe—*WHHHHAAAAAAA!* at that moment, before the last chorus."

On John Peel's *Something Else*, on television two months after the show at the Factory club, the song is speeded up, a way to keep the interest of listeners who have heard "Transmission" before, maybe of musicians who have played it too many times. It's automatic. The Doors were always hovering over Joy Division, as if watching them go to places they had glimpsed but never reached; far in front of the sound, Curtis never sounded so much like Jim Morrison, somewhat distracted, forgetting where he is, then remembering, clumsy, then rushing, as if he's trying to run right out of the song.

The song catches up, and traps him at just that point where it tips into uncertainty. "When the going gets tough—" When the going gets tough, you find out how feeble you really are. Paradoxically, your voice gets louder, your body more violent, because arguments, ideas, even words, are now useless, and your voice, as a sound, and your body, as movement, are all you have. Curtis stares into the face of the BBC camera, his own face transparent, his eyes shaking in their sockets, the notion that this is Ian Curtis, famous person, Existential hero, *La Nausée* on two legs, falling far short of a person wordlessly asking, *Where am I, who are these people, why are they looking at me?*

Three years after he appeared as Ian Curtis in *Control*, Sam Riley played Pinkie in a remake of *Brighton Rock*. Graham Greene's 1938 novel was set in the thirties, as was the 1947 film with Richard Attenborough as the small-time gangster —the killer who marries a waitress, Rose, because she's a witness and now she'll keep her mouth shut. But as Sam Riley steps out onto the Brighton pier, it's 1964, with the Mods and Rockers about to take over the town and fight with knives and chains over the definition of cool.

Riley's face is squashed. "His brain is squirmin' like a toad," as Jim Morrison sang in "Riders on the Storm"— that's what Riley's Pinkie looks like. He is not as inhuman as Attenborough's, or as smart—behind his own thoughts, his own gestures of disdain, contempt, impatience, loathing, you can see him worry, for a second, over the things about himself he doesn't understand, and then you can see him decide he doesn't care.

In the crucial scene, just after Pinkie and Rose are married, in a squalid little civil ceremony, they're walking on the Brighton pier. "Rose stopped him," Greene wrote. "'Look,' she said, won't you give me one of those? As a souvenir. They don't cost much,' she said, 'only sixpence.' It was a small glass box like a telephone cabinet. 'Make a record of your own voice,' the legend ran." "'What do you want me to say?' 'Just anything,' she said. 'Say something to me. Say Rose and—something.'" Pinkie goes in, reads the instructions: "He looked over his shoulder and there outside she was watching him, with a smile. He saw her as a stranger: a shabby child from Nelson Place . . . He put in a sixpence, and speaking in a low voice for fear it might carry beyond the box, he gave his message up to be graven on vulcanite: 'God damn you, you little bitch, why can't you go back home forever and leave me be?'" They don't have a record player; it's a keepsake, she isn't going to hear it. Richard Attenborough's record is worse: "You asked me to make a record of me voice," he says, looking like Richard Widmark in the same year in *Kiss of Death*, the two movies playing as the world's ugliest double feature. "Well, here it is. What you want me to say is, I love you"—romantic music comes up as Rose gazes adoringly through the glass—"Well, here's the truth. I hate you, you little slut. You make me sick. Why don't you get back to Nelson Place and leave me be?"

Sam Riley's Pinkie and Andrea Riseborough's Rose are

on the pier. She asks him for a record. He brushes her off. With people passing by, she screams at him: "If you don't want me then why don't you just leave me alone? What do you want me for?" People are staring. Pinkie is scared: this whole thing is about keeping him safe, respectable, out of prison. "I'd rather drown!" Rose says. "You can have your record," he says. He says it again. She smiles at him. She apologizes. He goes into the booth, with Rose smiling and waving through the glass.

Riley puts in a coin, and the machine places a 45 blank on the turntable. He looks down at it, his face serious and dark, as if he's about to testify in court, to speak just before he is sentenced, to make his final, defiant statement, his final, pathetic plea. The words he speaks are not that different from what Greene's or Attenborough's Pinkie says, but as speech they are in a different language. As Attenborough played him, Pinkie carried a patina of urbanity and an air of confidence. Riley catches all the years of privation since the economic ruin of the 1930s, the bombing of England in the 1940s, the postwar rationing of Pinkie's childhood, a school class system that divides the worthy from the worthless except for those in places where no one is ever judged worthy, a coarsening of affect that has spread through the whole of British life, a longing for style that was just about to explode with the Beatles, Brian Epstein, Julie Christie, Peter Blake, Joe Meek, Lindsay Anderson, the Rolling Stones, Robert

Fraser, Joe Orton, the Who, Carnaby Street, Tom Stoppard, Ray Davies, Terence Stamp, Peter Sellers, David Bailey, Michael Caine, Mary Quant, Joseph Losey, Twiggy, Tom Courtenay, Dirk Bogarde, Susannah York, Marianne Faithfull, or for that matter Christine Keeler, Johnny Edge, and the nightclub gangsters the Kray twins, who at one point plotted to blackmail Brian Epstein into surrendering the Beatles—an explosion that for this Pinkie would come just too late.* Even in the 1960s, the '30s are breathing through his pores.

*About the time Reggie and Ronnie Kray sat for David Bailey and were lionized by certain pop stars, at least from a distance, they met the Beatles' manager in a gay bar, and formed a plan to seize control of the Beatles by threatening to expose Epstein as a homosexual. As Ronnie Kray wrote in 1993 in his autobiography, *My Story*, "The Beatles and the Rolling Stones were rulers of pop music, Carnaby Street ruled the fashion world . . . and me and my brother ruled London." In 1968 they were convicted of double murder and sentenced to life—but the notion of taking over the Beatles was not as crazy as it might seem. In 2000, Paul McCartney told the story of how Epstein, near the end of his life and consumed with a despair he could not put into words, tried to sell the Beatles to the music mogul Robert Stigwood, a king of shlock with whom he had already merged his umbrella company, NEMS Enterprises: "We said, 'Well, let's just get this straight. We're not going to be sold to anyone. If you can do it, you can continue to manage us. We love you. We're not going to be sold. In fact, if you do, if you somehow manage to pull this off, we can promise you one thing. We will record "God Save the Queen" for every single record we make from now on and we'll sing it out of tune. That's a promise. So if this guy buys us that's what he's buying.'

"Funnily enough," McCartney said, "the Sex Pistols did it years later. It was always a good idea."

"You asked me to make a record of my voice," Riley says. "Well, here it is."

There is the faint, gravelly spindle sound of the record turning.

"What you want me to say is"—and Riley's voice turns like the record with disgust—"I love you. Well, I don't. I hate you"—and his voice burrs through *hate* with its own wind.

Outside the booth, Rose might be sensing what is happening; she looks alarmed.

"I hate the way you look," Pinkie says, bearing down. "I hate the way you talk—I hate everything about you." Rose smiles again. "You make me sick."

Riley's Pinkie stares at the spinning 45 as if it's a mirror. He's becoming aware of himself as an artist; this is now a performance, an art statement that will live on outside of him. He is making a record.

"Goddamn you little bitch, why don't you go back to where you came from and leave me alone forever?"

It comes off the screen as the first punk single. That Riley has already played Ian Curtis, that anyone watching *Brighton Rock* in 2010 has likely already seen Riley embrace punk and take it past itself, is part of this: though in ordinary time *Brighton Rock* comes three years after *Control*, in the historical time of the two films, *Brighton Rock* is taking place some twelve, thirteen, fourteen years earlier. But a more swirling time is at play: time made by the dictum that, as the singer David Thomas puts it, the ballad gets what the ballad wants. It is a curving time made by the way actors carry roles with them through their careers, each role, if the actors can burn at the core, bleeding into every other; it's pop time, the time made by the way songs and movies cannibalize history and rewrite it according to a logic of their own. In this time, where what Sam Riley learned singing Ian Curtis's songs informs every syllable coming out of his Pinkie's mouth, with the disgust of Curtis's "Dance, dance, dance" thudding against Pinkie's *I hate, I hate, I hate,* Sam Riley's Pinkie is his own father. That is, he is Ian Curtis's father, and Rose his mother, playing that record for him all through his childhood, saying, "Listen, this is your father's voice."

In 1964 in *Brighton Rock,* Pinkie is killed. Rose, in a home for unwed or abandoned expectant mothers, is at her bed in an ugly dormitory. Another girl has a birthday; she gets a little portable record player. When everyone is asleep, Rose brings the record player to her bed, plugs it in, and, cradling it in her arms, plays her own record for the first time. "You've asked me to make a record of my voice," she hears. "Well, here it is. What you want me to say is, I love you." But the grooves are cheap; the needle sticks. "*I love you.*" "*I love you.*" "*I love you.*" "*I love you*" — the record won't play beyond those words. Those words are all she'll ever hear, but her son will hear the music.

In the
Still of
the Nite

1956·1959·2010

Four deep, rumbling bass notes on a piano fall into a full *oooooo* from voices so bound as one they feel more like the sound of a horn than people, individuals, people with names, desires, intentions, ambitions, fears—a sound more like nature than will. The sound is muffled, made of its own echo, from a cave in the imagination, far away, something always present and always just out of reach, until this moment, which lasts only a single second before it disappears into a song. It's enough to say that something all out of proportion to its medium—a seven-inch 45, a transistor radio—is already under way.

It's 19 February 1956 in New Haven, Connecticut, where Fred Parris, tenor, and three other singers—Al Denby and Ed Martin, baritones, and Jim Freeman, bass—are recording as the Five Satins. They'd recorded before—the previous summer, when there really were five of them. Two teenagers who convinced Parris they could make records, Marty Kugell and Tom Sokira, took the singers to the New Haven VFW post. The musicians the producers had hired never appeared; that day, the Five Satins sang acappella. For one song, "Rose Mary," Kugell and Sokira had instruments overdubbed for a single on their own Standord label; for the flipside, "All Mine," they never got around to it, though with

the two-track tape recorder they were using, the faint rumble of a passing truck, like a phantom bass player, was never
erased, leaving a sound that on the record itself you could
less hear than apprehend. It was a tangled doo-wop ballad,
but at the very end, with nothing to fall back upon, Parris
stepped out of genre, fashion, fad, out of a song anyone else
could have written and anyone else could have sung. "This
is the story," he announced—and with those four words he
instantly gave the song that had preceded them a drama it
hadn't been able to produce, a sense of foreboding after the
fact, because until this moment, though you might have
heard what happened, you didn't care—"of a love affair."
There was a pause, and then an incantation, as full of pride
as anguish: "*Mine, mine, mine, mine, mine—*"

Parris was no amateur. As a seventeen-year-old late of the
Canaries—for a long moment it seemed impossible to name
a group harmony combo after anything but a bird—he was
writing his own songs. He formed the Scarlets, and traveled
to New York to get a record deal. Starting in 1954 with "Dear
One," they made three singles for Bobby Robinson's Red
Robin label. Robinson was a major operator, at the center of
the Harlem hit parade, but none of the records made it out
of town. There was one hit—Parris's "Cry Baby," which did
nothing for the Scarlets, but in 1956 made it to number 18
on the national charts in an utterly bleached version by the
Bonnie Sisters, three nurses from Bellevue Hospital. Parris

went back to New Haven. He and the rest of the Scarlets were drafted, scattered around the country; Parris formed the Five Satins in New Haven during a leave. Of course their Standord single went nowhere. But one night, as Parris always told the story, on guard duty in Philadelphia, thinking about his girlfriend, he wrote "In the Still of the Nite."

Not "In the Still of the Night"—both Cole Porter and Hoagy Carmichael and Jo Dent had written sweeping dance numbers with that title in the thirties. This was simple—

In the still
Of the night

—but with a hesitation that made the memory the song was attempting to summon almost too sweet, too erotic, to bear—

I held you—
Held you tight

—it wasn't obvious. Once past those rumbling piano notes, the listener, like the singer, held on to every word.

Kugell and Sokira had backing musicians this time—a pianist, a stand-up bass player, a drummer—but no money for a place to record, and they didn't want to go back to the VFW. As Parris told Randall Beach of the *New Haven Reg-*

ister in 1980, "they made a deal with somebody" who could set them up in the basement of Saint Bernadette's Church, in the all-white Morris Cove section of New Haven, near the shoreline. "This 'somebody,' Parris said, also played saxophone," Beach wrote. "The 'deal' was that if he could get them in there, they would 'let him play sax on the record.'"

So they dove in, with Parris's aching lead and Denby, Freeman, and Martin mouthing doo-wops behind him: "Shoo-doot, shooby-doh, shoo-doot, shooby-doh, shoo-doot, *shooby*"—and then an unexpected "Whoa," a long, climbing syllable that seemed to soar out of earshot and took the performance into a realm of its own.

As the song went on, that sensual hesitation at the beginning disappeared, and everything was chaste, fated, in God's hands—and, as singing, almost everything was completely straight. Save for a slight tearing around the edges of the words, speaking for doubt, ambiguity, the sense that the love the song was chasing might already be gone, there was nothing in Parris's voice you would have been surprised to hear in any white nightclub in the United States. The singer remembered a night in May and the stars in the sky, he hoped and prayed that love would last. *"I remember,"* he called, letting the word rest in the air—just as he had so subtly and, as the song would resonate over the decades, so indelibly rhymed "May" and "Pray"—and the singers called the words back to him. There was a second, this time overtly

melodramatic hesitation just past a minute into the performance. "I'll hope/And I'll pray," Parris lilted, and then as he
broke "To keep" off the phrase, starkly, the pianist returned
to take the song back. He pounded twice, again that deep
bass rumble—

Bump bump

—the sound surrounded on each side by a silence so thick
you could feel the night closing in on it. Parris was on top
of the moment, barely letting go of one word and half of
another—

Your pre*h*—

—the word seemingly cut off right there, leaving you with
no idea of what might be coming next, and then the pianist
hit again,

Bump bump

—before Parris smoothly finished the word "precious" as if
it had always come in two parts, soaring again into the word
"love," the word itself now so in love with its own idea that it
rippled in widening concentric circles as if a stone had been
thrown into its lake.

But the song was lumbering; it was beginning to wear itself out. It's hard to say what keeps it alive—some promise of something more in the very incompleteness of the emotion the singer wants to fulfill, but can't? And then, as has happened so many times in rock 'n' roll, the instrumental break took the song past itself. The sound in early rock 'n' roll records, especially group harmony singles, often has a preternatural clarity at its heart; you are there, watching, hoping, as the song unfolds, that no one breaks the spell. The sound is open, full of room; you sense time passing. But this is not like that. On this night in the basement, there's a whole sky inside the sound, and the sky is overcast, the clouds thickening and descending as the song pushes forward, so that every expression of emotion, every moment of particularity, where the listener can sense that what is at issue is now, not then, here, not there, feels like a victory. There is no telling whether the record, the thing that goes on sale and on the radio, has captured a sound that once existed in that now, not then, or whether the record has imposed a sound on an event that had no such texture, but the sound is what remains: the record is the sound, the sound is the record. It is this darkening, desperate world that the sound both calls up and makes—and, as the guitarist and critic Robert Ray once said, "What's interesting about rock & roll is that the truly radical aspect occurs at the level of *sound*. 'Tutti Frutti' is far more radical than Lennon's 'Woman Is the Nigger of the

World,' and the sound of Bob Dylan's voice changed more people's ideas about the world than his political message did." And now this sound, too, will change people's ideas about the world—it will feel bigger, less fixed, more threatening, more beautiful—and it will change how people feel themselves to be in the world.

Again, the piano rises up out of the music, but distantly now, claiming nothing, setting the stage. Vinny Mazzetta, the Saint Bernadette's connection, raises his saxophone and begins to play. Denby, Freeman, and Martin take over the singing. *Doo-bop, doo-bah*, they sing under Mazzetta's bending solo, the sound of someone completely lost in a song, in a nowhere Parris has not yet found, a utopia where there are no dreams to realize, no debts to pay, where there is only reverie, where for a few seconds every dream is fulfilled and every debt forgiven, and Mazzetta and the singers floated through time as if it wasn't there: "It just came out," Mazzetta said in 2010. "I played what I felt." The singers gained in passion with each repetition, *Doo-bop, DOO-BAH, doo-bop, DOO-BAH*, then a single *doo-bop* cut off, suspending the moment, time not stopping but pushing back, the halt calling everything into question. Mazzetta keeps on, in a world of his own, and again the singers cast their fate with his. The piano steps in again, Parris again takes the song, but after only a few seconds he sings the title words for the last time and begins a wordless drift, a long, high walk into the territory Mazzetta had found that Parris can now see and trust, and so he left everyone—the other singers, the musicians, whoever might hear him—behind. Years later I called up a DJ who had talked all through that closing passage, complaining that it was the best part, that he'd ruined the song. That's what endings like that were for, he said: for DJs to sell the next record, the next commercial, to keep you from changing the station as a song faded out. And you didn't change it, he said, did you?

With the original Standord release it was the B-side, "The Jones Girl," a fast number credited to Jim Freeman, that first got airplay, and the same was true with the re-release for a wider market on the New York label Ember. But "The Jones Girl" dried up with a few plays, and some DJs turned the record over. "In the Still of the Nite" wasn't a huge hit—not right away. In 1956 it climbed no higher than number 24. But it took up residence in people's hearts. When in 1959 the Los Angeles DJ Art Laboe assembled the first *Oldies But Goodies* collection on his own Original Sound label, "In the Still of the Nite" was the opening track. It had only been three years, but to the song's original teenage listeners that was a lifetime, and the *Oldies But Goodies* album carried a queer sensation, that of feeling your own life historicized, given weight, a promise that if the things one loved were, like all things, certain to pass away, it wouldn't be that quickly. The album and those that followed did more: they gave rock 'n' roll as such a sense of its own history, which meant a suspicion that it might have a future.

Over the years, "In the Still of the Nite" sold millions of copies. Included on soundtrack albums for *American Graffiti* and *Dirty Dancing*, it orbited the globe like a satellite. Though he continued to record new songs well into the 1980s, Parris and different versions of the Five Satins never played a show, whether in clubs around New Haven, for rock 'n' roll revival concerts in New York, on PBS doo-wop fund-raisers, without "In the Still of the Nite" being the reason the audience was there at all.

With those in the audience now silently taking the place of the backing singers, the song never lost its luster, or its fundamental unlikelihood, the aura of accident and chance that seeped into the performance. It could, and did, go anywhere: at first, into slow dances, girls resting their heads on boys' shoulders even if the girls were taller, and then, decades later, when the song had to let people change it if it was to survive, into the threesome in David Cronenberg's *Dead Ringers*. One of Jeremy Irons's two suicidal, sadomasochistic twin gynecologists is dancing with a woman; the song creeps out of the expensive darkness of the room. The woman demands that the other twin, sitting on a couch, looking as if he would rather be anywhere else, dance too. He resists; she insists; he pulls himself to his feet. With the woman in the middle, the two men grasp her body, but really they are reaching for each other, enacting her annihilation as she moves between them, each of them wishing she were dead. For an instant, there is the sense that the song could actually save them all. Then the two men, both with that sick Jeremy Irons look of loathing for all existence, kill it. Why was the song there? Because it was just right for the scene as Cronenberg wrote it? Or because he had always loved the song, and had waited years for the chance to play it himself, in his own way?

That was 1988, almost as many years after the Five Satins made "In the Still of the Nite" as have passed since Cronenberg made his austere and nearly perfect film, and in those years the record has lived a fuller life. "You could tell I was only 21," Vinny Mazzetta told Randall Beach in 2010. "I didn't know any better: bringing blacks into the Cove, into a church. But I just said, 'They're here to make a record.' A good thing happened."

Sometime in the late fifties, the Spades, a vocal group that formed in 1957 at McCallum High School in Austin—with no White-Negro hipster ambitions, they would claim, let alone any racial disparagement ("The playing card theme," one member said. "You'd have names like the Diamonds, the Knaves, the Kings and so on")—took up the song. For vocal groups, it had become what "Louie Louie" would be for guitar bands in the 1960s and long after that: something to get a rehearsal started, something to test yourself against. Right off, it had been covered by such hitmakers as the Fleetwoods and the Crests, both of whom succeeded in making it sound ordinary. What the Spades did with it might have been what any number of groups anywhere in the country did with it, but the Spades left something behind.

Don Burch and Tommy Kaspar were eighteen and John Goeke sixteen when they began singing together; Jimmy Davis joined later. They were the first signing for Domino Records, a company that was started after eleven Austin business people attended a seminar called "How to Market a Song." In 1958, a single, "Baby," attracted the major label Liberty in Los Angeles, which took over distribution. To avoid alienating anybody, now that they were playing on a bigger stage, the group changed its name to the Slades. When the Texas stations playing the Slades' second single, Burch's "You Cheated," were flooded with calls, the Domino partners decided to hold onto it—but their seminar hadn't included pointers on how to meet unexpected demand or to break into major markets, which is to say to include a bribery expense for big city DJs and station managers in the promotion budget. In Los Angeles, the producer George Motola leaped into the breach. With cash in hand, he surveyed the fabulously polyglot doo-wop and R&B world of the city, took the best—the songwriter and crooner Jesse Belvin, the harmony singers Mel Williams and Charlie Wright, the older blues singer Frankie Ervin, plus Johnny "Guitar" Watson—named them the Shields, as close as he could get to the Slades, put them in the studio, and watched them leave the Slades in the dust, scoring a national hit while the original slipped off the charts and disappeared. It was a matter of fresh-faced Texas boys and tough L.A. hustlers, white boys finding their voices in what had begun as a black style and then black artists, some of whom had been making records all through the fifties, taking their song and showing the kids who'd made it up how it was done. Over Ervin's stolid, deliberate lead on Burch's blunt lyric—

You cheated
You lied

—with Williams and Wright deepening the Slades' measured Judgment Day doo-wop chorus, Belvin, in a ghostly, wordless falsetto, floated over the music, swam through it, lifted the song into the air it would soon occupy all over the country.

It was how pop magic worked. You took something ordinary, in this case Frankie Ervin's voice, which betrayed his thirty-two years, all the groups he'd joined and left, all the records his voice had marked without credit or more money than might last the day or the week, and linked it to something that seemed not quite real—here, the ghost the song as its writer shaped it never knew it had. You let the plainness of one part of the music throw what was beautiful, what was strange, into relief, but you never let the light in the sound blind the real people marching through it. You kept the magic just out of reach, a receding element that made you come back for more, certain that, the next time, you could catch it in your hand. And it was here—Jesse Belvin finding the real song in what it didn't or couldn't say, making Frankie Ervin sound square as he dutifully walked through the lyric, just as with the backing vocals in "In the Still of the Nite" finally taking the song from Fred Parris's plummy lead, Parris himself had escaped the prison of correct singing in his embrace of the wordless wail—that the soul music of the next decades began. The music of what, if it was to be music at all, had to be there—the music of what you couldn't see. "Jesse'd write these songs but actually all he might have were six words on a piece of paper," Belvin's friend Gaynel Hodge said in 1986, talking about how Belvin sold songs. "He'd go into the record companies and start singing, just making up shit, and hypnotise them with his voice because he had such a strong effect on people when he sang. But after he left with his money, the people would realize the song had been all Jesse and all they were left with was smoke."

The Slades kept trying. They all but covered themselves with Burch's "You Gambled." With the hard-nosed New

Orleans singer Joyce Harris drafted for a day, they answered themselves with "I Cheated." Eventually Domino Records closed up shop and the Slades went on to real life. Near the end of their story, in 1959 or 1960, they spent an afternoon in their rehearsal space. The sound on the tapes they made that day is suppressed, narrow, staticky—you can picture one mike in a metal shed. They were doing warm-up exercises, loosening their fingers and vocal chords, opening their chests on the Crows' 1954 "Gee Whiz," the Five Keys' 1955 "Ling Ting Tong," the Casuals' 1957 "So Tough," the Elegants' 1958 "Little Star," the Bell Notes' 1959 "I've Had It." There was nothing special, nothing to suggest how close they came—as close as *American Bandstand*, all the way to Philadelphia to mime "You Cheated," only to have it fall to the Shields' version on the same show the very next day, for that matter to have their song turn up on the rockabilly singer Ronnie Hawkins's *Mr. Dynamo* not two years later, but credited to one Levon Helm, Hawkins's teenage drummer —nothing special, except for "In the Still of the Nite."

It's a once-in-a-lifetime performance. In Don Burch's straining lead, with the rest pushing their doo-wops in front of him and a single acoustic guitar keeping time, you can hear someone driving past his own limits: as a singer, but also as a person consumed by desire and terrified of loss. The song is revealing someone who wasn't there before. The song isn't telling him what to do or what to feel; he is reaching for this song because, suddenly, more so with each phrase, he needs to say what it says. His voice is thin, reedy, tailing off the last words of the lines, the words standing out in a new way, with *still* threatening and harsh, *night* open, beckoning, a garden under the moon—and when he reaches the last "night," the last word of the song, he won't let it go. He caresses the word, lets it fall slowly through his fingers like sand, watching the last grains glisten as they fall, each one its own true note.

With the second verse, Burch adds something to the song that was never there before this day, and never after it. "I remember, that night in May," he sings, "When you kissed me"—and the hesitation that caught Fred Parris in the first verse now catches Burch. He double-pumps on "When," letting the word fragment into two parts, and then rushes across the line, letting it shudder through him. He puts everything he has into the four words of the line, and it sweeps him up. "I could hear you say"—but he never says what she said. Maybe he was too consumed by the moment to hear more than the sound of her voice.

The way Burch puts an event into the song—*you kissed me*—something physical, intimate, irreducible—is shocking. Suddenly this is not just a song. Someone is telling you what happened to him, and you believe him—as pain floods over him, you have to believe him. The girl in the song is present, and he is not just sitting in his room, dreaming of what almost happened, something he wants so much he can almost believe it did happen: "Oh I couldn't sleep / For on my mind / Was the image / Of a girl / I hope to find," as the Safaris put it in 1960, embarrassing a good part of the nation as they did so. *When you kissed me* — it's a moment that can't be taken back. "What you do to me, baby, it never gets out of me," Geeshie Wiley sang in 1930 in "Last Kind Words Blues"; that's where, that day in Austin, life found Don Burch, or the person he was able to become when he sang "In the Still of the Nite."

A half-century after that afternoon rehearsal, the *Wall Street Journal* ran a piece titled "Should Bob Dylan Retire?" "When to Leave the Stage," ran the subhead: "A generation of music icons is hitting retirement age, along with their baby boomer fans. Is it time for Bob Dylan to hang up his hat and harmonica?" "The issue of whether Mr. Dylan should pack it in has been an enduring parlor game in music circles," John Jurgensen wrote. "Most alarming to listeners devoted to his seminal recordings: the state of Mr. Dylan's voice, decades on from its first signs of deterioration. Dr. Lee Akst, director of the Johns Hopkins Voice Center, says it's impossible to diagnose Mr. Dylan without examination, but . . . " Illustrating the piece was a remake of the cover of Dylan's second album, *The Freewheelin' Bob Dylan,* with the singer and his girlfriend Suze Rotolo hugging his arm as they walked through the snow on a New York street, shining with the pleasure of being in the right place at the right time, embodying youth, love, sex, freedom, and possibility, and so fully that the single block of Jones Street in Greenwich Village in 1963 could open onto every highway and back road in the United States. But now you saw a man and woman from behind. He was heavy and his hair was white; she leaned into him as before, thick and stooped, holding onto her walker in the slick of slush on the pavement. The story was bizarre from its premise: the notion that it was up to the public to decide when Bob Dylan or anybody else should "leave the stage"—which really meant shut up, or die. The subtext was the presentation of age as a disease you could catch if you got too close—something to turn away from, something decent people should not have to look at, as the figures on the album now titled *The No Longer Freewheelin' Bob Dylan* acknowledged, turning their faces away from the viewers' gaze, sparing them their disgust. Suze Rotolo died less than three months after the story appeared; Fred Parris, enormous, his features locked in place, was still singing "In the Still of the Nite." Jesse Belvin never had to worry about it. He died in a car crash on 5 February 1960, after a show in Little Rock with Little Willie John and Jackie Wilson.

Some months before the *Wall Street Journal* ran its story, the Slades gathered in what looked like a locker room to rehearse for their own appearance on a PBS doo-wop special. Two of the four were fat; they were all bald. They sang "You Cheated," and then they sang "In the Still of the Nite." Tommy Kaspar did not allow himself even the slightest change of expression as he carefully picked the strings of his guitar through his backing vocal; John Goeke and Jimmy Davis bore down as well. Don Burch, his guitar far out in front of his body, resting on his huge stomach, his eyes smiling, made his way through the song like a swimmer without a doubt in his mind that he'd make it to shore. He didn't sing "When she kissed me." As the other Slades chanted "I remember" around him, maybe that was something he didn't.

All I
Could Do
Was Cry

2013·1960·2008

In early 2013 Beyoncé bestrode America as a colossus. On January 21, at Barack Obama's second inauguration, following James Taylor's rendition of "America the Beautiful," Kelly Clarkson's of "My Country 'Tis of Thee," a strong inaugural address, a poem by Richard Blanco, and a benediction by the Reverend Luis León, she closed the ceremonies with "The Star-Spangled Banner." Less than two weeks later, on February 3, she took the halftime show at the Super Bowl. She was inescapable, a pop image so overwhelming that the person inside of it seemed not unreal but beyond reality, and beyond criticism. When the *New Yorker* columnist George Packer wrote that her Super Bowl performance left him "a bit cold—a highly polished combination of corporate marketing and pole dancing," the scent of failure came off the words. You could feel that he had demeaned himself, not her.

These are official historical events, now folded into the official American story. As they happened, they echoed endlessly off the sides of the American mountain. "America the Beautiful" is unendurable to begin with; James Taylor's autumn-leaves stroll through the number could have been a recruiting video for a second-rank New England prep school, if not Austen Riggs. "I have to admit, this shows how far we have come as a nation," Stephen Colbert said that night, appearing as the right-wing talk show host he has played on *The Colbert Report* since 2006, the year he appeared at the White House Correspondents' annual dinner to eviscerate both attending President George W. Bush and the toadying White House press corps itself. "A black guy who likes James Taylor! 'Cause I've seen fire and I've seen rain,'" he crooned, "'but I've never seen a black guy at your shows.'" Suddenly Barack Obama turned into Steve Martin in his "I was born a poor black child" standup routine, explaining how as a white foundling he was raised by a family of black sharecroppers, only discovering his true self—not as a white person, but as a music lover—when, as a young man, he heard Montovani for the first time. It was a parable of American identity restaged most expansively in Martin's film *The Jerk*, in 1979, with the family gathered around their radio:

> " . . . and that concludes this Sunday night Gospel Hour, live from the Four Square Gospel Church at the Divine Salvation in St. Louis, Missouri, the Reverend Willard Willman, Pastor. And now, music throughout the night. Music in a mellow mood."
>
> "Don't touch that radio! Don't touch it! Turn it up! Turn it up! I've never heard music like this before! It speaks to me! Taj! Dad! This is unbelievable . . . If this is out there, think of how much more is out there! This is the kind of music that tells me to go out there and be somebody!"

"My Country 'Tis of Thee" was the song Martin Luther King, Jr., seized on the steps of the Lincoln Memorial on 28 August 1963: "And this will be the day—this will be the day when all of God's children will be able to sing with new meaning, 'My country 'tis of thee. Sweet land of liberty. Of thee I sing. Land where my fathers died, land of the pilgrims' pride. From every—mountainside, let freedom ring' and if America is to be a great nation, this must become true." There was no pause at all between the last word of the song and the *and if* that followed, suspending America's greatness between past and future, a future America might never serve. As King spoke, his own words entered the song, and Kelly Clarkson appeared to be listening to the song, and hearing that story telling itself within it, as she sang.

She had to follow Aretha Franklin, who had performed the song at Barack Obama's first inauguration, and she didn't shame herself. As she slowly turned the song toward a bigger and bigger presence, she was both a star and self-effacing, commanding and modest. Moving into the forgotten third verse, then the fourth, she made the country start, saying, *There is so much we don't know, there is so much to remember.*

> Let music swell the breeze,
> And ring from all the trees,
> Sweet freedom's song;
> Let mortal tongues awake;

Let all that breathe partake;
Let rocks their silence break,
The sound prolong.

Joe Biden looked shocked, and thrilled. You couldn't tell whether he hadn't heard the verse Clarkson sang before, or if he hadn't heard her before.

Beyoncé closed the show; swathed against the cold in clothes that looked like extensions of her blonde hair, of her aura, she did the National Anthem as a show-closer, drawing attention to her own gorgeousness. Near the end she raised her left hand in the gesture of an orator emphasizing a point; the gesture was so much more that of a politician than of a singer it let you imagine she was inaugurating herself. As the song ended she remade it into the last number of some quasi-historical-religious Hollywood epic, *Ben-Hur* if not *Les Misérables*: "Brave, brave — *the Brave!*" Back in the real world, Beyoncé and her husband, the hip-hop emperor Jay-Z, seated behind her, made up almost as big a power couple as Hillary and Bill Clinton; that night, according to the next day's news, she danced until three at the White House with the president. But as a show-closer this was also a warm-up.

With a $50 million contract with Pepsi, with her face on the cover of *Vogue* and half a dozen other magazines, with the ghost of Vince Lombardi providing a voice-over that kicked off the performance less as a pole dance than a Tony Robbins rally—"The will to excel, the will to win, these are the things that endure"—at her Pepsi-sponsored Super Bowl show Beyoncé appeared on a pedestal as her own statue. She brought herself to life as her own Pygmalion, breathing into her own mouth. Throwing off the restraint of the inauguration, she plunged into the melismatics that turn every song into a mirror into which the singer gazes at her own beauty. From her first records with Destiny's Child—the group brought back together for this night—through her long string of number-one hits, "Crazy in Love," "Baby Boy," "Check on It," "Irreplaceable," "Single Ladies (Put a Ring on It)," she followed in the footsteps of Whitney Houston and Mariah Carey in replacing even a memory of soul music with its counterfeit. The transformation is magical in its completeness. What used to be called worrying a line—in the old sense of the word, where to worry something, a singer with a fragment of a song, a writer with a sentence, a child with a nail or a piece of wood for a toy, was to move something back and forth, up and down, until it gave up its true meaning, or even, as singing, revealed that the singer would never reach that final truth, but dramatizing how close he or she came—was erased by its fraud.

Worrying also meant just that—that you could hear the singer worrying that he or she would not be able to get across what he or she was trying to say, that the singer would fail not

only him or herself, but the listener and the song. Otis Redding pushed it farthest: in "Try a Little Tenderness," "These
Arms of Mine," and "I've Been Loving You Too Long," worrying a line dramatized a contract between the singer, the
song, and the listener.

The contract was that each would give what they had;
that each would try, the singer speaking as he or she sang,
the song speaking as it was sung, the listener speaking as he
or she listened, to mean what they said. You could imagine,
as you listened, that as the singer changed the song, the song
changed the singer, and you could imagine that both would
change you. Nothing would be left the same.

Some forms of music spark the freedom of singers to say,
in words or how words are sung, in pace, hesitation, timbre, shouts, or silences, what they most deeply and desper-
ately want to say; other forms take it away. The essence of
melisma after soul music was captured in a comment by the
presidential historian Rick Perlstein, writing about how, in
the 2012 campaign, for Mitt Romney a lie, hundreds upon
catalogued hundreds, in all forms, in all tones of voice, the
tiniest adding credence to the most profound, had changed
from a mere political trick into a form of discourse, from a
short con into, in Perlstein's words, a long con, the rules of
which were understood equally by both speaker and audience. "It's time," Perlstein said, "to consider whether Romney's fluidity with the truth is, in fact, a feature and not a

bug: a constituent part of his appeal to conservatives. The point here is not just that he lies when he says conservative things, even if he believes something different in his heart of hearts—but that lying is what makes you sound the way a conservative is supposed to sound, in pretty much the same way that curlicuing all around the note makes you sound like a contestant on *American Idol* is supposed to sound." Curlicuing around the note allows a singer to mimic the sense of event in soul music, the sense that something is happening which has not happened before and cannot be repeated, by mimicking the apprehension of soul, those moments when singers dramatize their struggle to bring out of themselves what lies buried in them, inaccessible, until this moment, even to themselves. As worrying is mimicked into melisma, it is also, behind the curtain of the effect, in a lie no one who tells it will ever admit to, satirized. What was once a sign of meaning what you said is transformed into a device by which singers communicate that they don't. Perhaps reaching its limit with Jennifer Hudson's performance of Al Green's "Let's Stay Together" to open the inaugural ball, with Barack and Michelle Obama beaming, or trying to keep a straight face, music shifts from a means by which one can signify that one is not faking emotional commitment to a means by which one can signify that one is. It goes back to gospel, both the technique and the soul. As the singer must convince you that as he or she sings, he or she has, by a commitment God can recognize, called down a visitation, then the tradition in which Beyoncé works is not merely bad music, but a form of blasphemy—though, unlike the outrage among devout African-Americans when Ray Charles or Sam Cooke or even Aretha Franklin used the gospel sound to sing about not God's love but that of men and women on earth, no one is offended. The opposite is true: as with Rick Perlstein's Romney, the falsity itself, felt and embraced, delivers its own kind of gratification, its own thrill.

That, at the Super Bowl, for nearly fourteen minutes, as in almost her entire career, was what Beyoncé had to say. She seemed someone entirely composed of money. Her gorgeousness was a concept, and as a concept it was automatic and finally bland. Unlike Elvis, Little Richard, the Beatles, Bob Dylan, Madonna, Tupac Shakur, Eminem, or Lady Gaga, she divided no one from anyone else. You didn't have to have an opinion about her; you only had to acknowledge her mastery, and it was impossible not to, even though the longer you looked, the less there was to see.

The first two words of Etta James's "All I Could Do Was Cry," from 1960, are the most devastating. She was born Jamesetta Hawkins in Los Angeles in 1938; at fifteen, living in San Francisco, she formed a vocal trio. Johnny Otis was in town with his band; after a hotel-room audition, James faked a permission note from her mother, lied about her age, with Otis went back to Los Angeles and cut an answer-record to Hank Ballard's huge hit "Work with Me Annie": "The Wallflower (Roll with Me Henry)," with the parenthetical changed to "Dance with Me" when DJs objected. In 1955 it was number 1 on the R&B charts for a solid month. As covered by the radio singer Georgia Gibbs, it was number 1 on the pop charts. James spent the next five years on the road, sharing stages with Little Richard, Bo Diddley, and Elvis Presley, writing songs, making more than a dozen singles, and falling farther into a barely adult oblivion, sleeping on buses, and learning the codes and disguises that came with marijuana, cocaine, and heroin: "I liked to see the needle stuck in the vein between hits," she wrote years later, with a double meaning that could have hung over most of her career. In 1960 she was hired at Chess Records in Chicago as a staff writer and singer. "All I Could Do Was Cry," her first single on her own for the company, was a number 2 R&B hit. The next year a version of "At Last," once a big-band hit for Glenn Miller with country-club vocals, now a chiming soul ballad, was another number 2—though over the years, as it reappeared in movies, TV commercials, covers by Celine Dion and other singers, it became an inescapable standard, and finally a self-erasing cliché, as if James had never done anything else, as if she'd never written "I'd Rather Go Blind."

"*IIIIIII* heard"—with a tone as rich and deep as any in rock 'n' roll, James doesn't so much sing the opening words of "All I Could Do Was Cry" as let them out, stones hidden in her lungs for twenty years. As the guitarist John Fahey once wrote of the first line of Hank Williams's "Alone and Forsaken"—"We met in the springtime"—"By the fifth word, you know it's all over," and here it only takes two. "It is enough to shrivel the heart to see," James Agee wrote of the last shots of Charlie Chaplin's *City Lights*, back-and-forth close-ups of the once-blind girl recognizing that her benefactor is not the rich man she imagined but the ruined, filthy tramp who now recognizes himself in her gaze, and this studied moment, in which the singer's whole life, her future as well as her past, seems to float behind her eyes as she sings, is the same.

James was twenty-two; she could have been sixty, or have lived a dozen lives without reaching twenty-three and re-membered all of them. "I heard church bells ringing," "All I Could Do Was Cry" begins; the singer's beloved is walking down the aisle with another woman. It's a hundred soap op-eras, a thousand other songs. Here the chorus is shapely and elegant, the verses off-balance, the "Earth Angel" triplets on guitar and piano an anachronism, the backing singers a distraction. None of it matters. *They met in the springtime*: in her first two words James is all sweep, fog rolling in over the hills in San Francisco and then all across the country, her tone so clear you can see straight through to the end of the song. As it goes on there are terrible, subtle shifts into a lower register, terrible because each degree of shading speaks for a despair that would shame anyone who tried to put it into words. She worries *hands* for only a second, but worlds of loss, of one hand coming away from another, never to touch again, are in that moment. She comes down harshly on certain words, pushing them away from her, trying to push the images they call up out of her mind. She seems to be remembering something that happened a long time ago, or imagining what's going to happen, and how she'll feel when she remembers it. Time stops, swirls, and fades out. *I heard*—James's sound is so full of beauty it's hard to stand it, and nothing that follows will even approach the purity of her sound, right here; it will draw you back to the song again and again, to see whether the spell will wear off, as you half hope it will, to see if the sound can again take you to unglimpsed countries in your own heart, which it will.

Etta James was not happy when in 2007 she heard that Beyoncé Knowles, born in 1981 in Houston, had been signed to play her in *Cadillac Records*, a film about Leonard Chess and the Chess label. "She's going to have a hill to climb, because Etta James ain't been no angel," she was quoted as saying. "I wasn't as bourgie as she is, she's bourgeois. She knows how to be a lady, she's like a model. I wasn't like that. I smoked in the bathroom at school." But the scene in

which Beyoncé records "All I Could Do Was Cry" is so powerful it can make the rest of her career seem like a cheat—a
cheat she played on herself, and her own talent, more than
anyone else.

Leonard Chess was born Lejzor Czyz in Poland in 1917;
along with his mother, his sister, and his brother and future
partner Phil, he arrived in the United States in 1928. After
the war he and his brother opened the Macombo, a blues
and jazz joint on the South Side in Chicago; by 1947 they
were in the record business. Muddy Waters put them on the
map; they effectively wiped every other label in town off of
it. Howlin' Wolf, Little Walter, Bo Diddley, Chuck Berry,
Sonny Boy Williamson, Buddy Guy, Dale Hawkins—for
the future members of the Rolling Stones, Fleetwood Mac,
and other British blues bands, the Chess studio at 2120 South
Michigan Avenue wasn't merely legendary, it was Shangri-
La. Leonard Chess died in 1969 at fifty-two, in his Cadillac,
of a heart attack, driving away from the offices of the company he had sold months before.

Cadillac Records is one thing after the other, all story and
no ambiance, no sense of place or purpose, until Beyoncé
appears. Off camera, we hear her singing, and Adrien Brody
as Leonard Chess calling "Cut, cut." "Fuck you," Beyoncé
says. "What the hell you know about the blues?" We see
them in the studio, Beyoncé in a short blonde Etta James
wig. James wasn't pretty; here neither is Beyoncé. "I gave

you a *damn* good track," she shouts, then closing her face with her eyes open, putting down the lead sheets. "You want it," she says matter-of-factly, "you sing it." Brody turns to the band, a what-can-you-do expression on his face. "Now she wants me to sing it. Now go home, go home. Forget it. Everybody go home. What you smilin' at?" He goes up to Beyoncé as she's gathering her things, and bears down on her like a mugger: "My mistake. You ain't woman enough for that song." "I'm plenty woman," Beyoncé says, and with the way her teeth fill her mouth for the second word, making *plenty* weight the line like an anchor, you begin to hear the music that wasn't there when the scene began. Brody presses harder, contempt covering his disgust. "That song's about being in love, you know what that is?" Beyoncé pulls into herself: "I know about love," she says with an absence of inflection that tells you you don't want to know what she knows. "Yeah?" says Brody, and now he's enjoying himself; he might have gotten out of bed this morning just for the chance to say what he's going to say. "Motherfucker ever walk out on you? Huh? Huh? Fucking not only walk out on you, but takin' another broad down the aisle?" Beyoncé's face as she walks away from him, as he stalks her around the studio, is blank, ugly, going dead. "Know what that feels like, baby? Huh?"

It's the storied George Goldner move. As a producer and record man he was as creative a force in the beginnings of the new music as anyone else—"There would have been no rock & roll without him," Phil Spector said when Goldner died, in 1970. Just months before, Goldner told the *Rolling Stone* writer Langdon Winner the story of how he got Arlene Smith, the seventeen-year-old lead singer of the Bronx quintet the Chantels, to do what she did—to go into the depths of doo-wop ballads like a maiden sacrificing herself to volcano gods. Winner had published a retrospective review of *The Chantels*, issued on Goldner's End label in 1958, raving about Arlene Smith: "What's so great about her voice? Well, to be frank, it starts where all other voices in rock stop . . . When she reaches for a high note she just keeps going. There is never a hint of strain. Nothing drops out. Her tone expands in breadth to match the requirements of high pitch . . . Like a three-thousand dollar stereo system playing Beethoven's Ninth, the highs, lows and mid range extend into infinity."

"Shortly after the review appeared," Winner wrote me in 2013, "I received a telephone call from George Goldner, legendary New York City record producer and businessman who'd recorded a number of early R&B, doo-wop and rock groups including the Chantels. He said he was coming to San Francisco on business and invited me to dinner. During a two-hour conversation, Goldner told a number of marvelous stories about Frankie Lymon and the Teenagers, the Crows, the Flamingos, and other groups he'd produced over the years. It was clear that he was happy to be getting some notice in the pages of *Rolling Stone* and wanted to make sure he was receiving sufficient credit for his contributions to rock and roll. At one point, for example, he proudly explained that the 'boy' celebrated in the Ad Libs' 1965 hit 'The Boy from New York City' was actually he himself.

"Eventually," Winner went on, "I asked Goldner about the extraordinary intensity in Arlene Smith's vocals. 'Obviously, she has a great natural ability and control of her voice,' I said. 'But she sings in a way that often seems right on the brink of emotional break down. Where did that come from?' 'You see,' he said, 'the Chantels were always very well prepared and sang beautifully. The first take of any of their songs was usually just about perfect. But I realized what a phenomenal talent Arlene Smith was. I wanted to push her to reach for something more. My strategy was to record two or three takes of a song and then storm out of the booth and start ranting. "This is horrible! Your singing today is lifeless, sloppy. Haven't you been rehearsing? We're just wasting our time here! What the hell's the matter with you?" I'd look Arlene right in the eye and yell at her until she was nearly in tears, and then finally say, "OK, I give up. Let's try it again." The next cut was always the one I was looking for. The edge you hear in her voice, the tone of desperation approaching hysteria is what I was trying to pull out of her. And sometimes I succeeded.'"

He had her where he wanted her, with no defenses left, ready to do anything to get away from this terrible man, and so she sang "If You Try" one more time, with every word with an *ay* sound in it exploding into the sky in pain and loss. As "*pray* for" and "*make* love" let you hear everything she will never have in life, she could be Ronald Colman in *Lost Horizon* finally making it back through the mountains to his Shangri-La, his eyes blinded by the paradise that you can't quite believe, even though it is within sight, he will ever reach again.

In Chicago, Beyoncé raises her head. She looks Brody in the eye, glances at the band, asks for one more take. Brody waves a dismissive yes. "Take fifteen," says an engineer off camera. The guitar and the piano hit a single note, and Beyoncé approaches the mike like an actress about to deliver a soliloquy. For a moment she pushes to the edge of melisma, then falls back into the song. This is not about her. The purpose of her performing the song, now, is not to draw attention to herself, her name, her story, but to inhabit the fictional character in the song, finding her story, her voice. "The song has me in church while watching my man marry someone else," James wrote in her autobiography. "I play the part of the lady left out, scorned, and wronged. 'For them life has just begun,' I sing as rice is thrown over their heads, 'and mine is at an end.' I sang like I meant it, and maybe I did. Maybe I foresaw the future. In the near future,

I'd get to live the very song I was singing . . . For the time being, though, I thought I was pretending, playacting, not knowing I was really playing the fool."

As she stands at the mike, Beyoncé half-slumps to one side, as if she's not singing but doing manual labor. Brody watches, smoking. Beyoncé's face goes back and forth between defiance of him and living in the song. As Muddy Waters, Jeffrey Wright stands in the control room, listening, smoking. As Beyoncé goes up high to a "Whoa-oh-oh-oh-oh"—which is a burst in the song, a hump in the music she has to get over, with no guarantee that she will, Wright smiles. She moves roughly, without grace. Whatever glamour she might have brought to the scene when she was dressed and made up for it is gone, erased by the woman in the song she has now become. She gets to the last verse— "Annnnnnnnd now—the wedding is over"—and Wright is contemplative, thinking not about her, not about the performance, but about life. He looks troubled, remembering something he hasn't thought about for a long time. *"THE RICE,"* Beyoncé sings, *"THE RICE HAS BEEN THROWN!"* and Wright slowly closes his eyes and his eyebrows rise. My God. He wasn't expecting this.

Beyoncé, you can think, was—was expecting to produce just that response, not in the film, where closed eyes and raised eyebrows are part of the script, but in the theater, out in the world, when the movie is seen, in 2008, when it came and went with much notice and little business, or when someone might stumble on the scene online, or in some future format, long after the film, or even Beyoncé or Etta James, are forgotten.

Later in the movie, Beyoncé sang "At Last." Her version was released as a single, and won a Grammy for Traditional R&B Vocal. Etta James died in 2012 at seventy-three, bitter, along with many other things, that in 2009 it was Beyoncé, not she, who was invited to sing "At Last" at Barack Obama's first inaugural ball.

Crying, Waiting, Hoping

1959·1969

O ne morning in 2013 I walked into Cole Coffee in Oakland, California. The music they play is teasing, always on low, less Hank Williams than his ghost, a chirpy girl-group number that turned out to be Etta James, a primitive blues no one could identify. This day the song was typically distant, dim—the harder you listened, the more the dimness seemed built into the music, part of what it was trying to say. But it was also unmistakable—unmistakably the Beatles playing Buddy Holly's "Crying, Waiting, Hoping," from when or where there was no telling. It sounded fabulous. It was also completely spectral, as if it were a mishearing of something else entirely—as if what I thought I was hearing had never been recorded at all.

Buddy Holly walked into the room sideways. In terms of pure power he can't stand up to those with whom he's most often linked as founder of a new music: Elvis Presley, Little Richard, Bo Diddley, Chuck Berry. He recorded nothing as immediately overwhelming—nothing that so forced an absolute confrontation between performer and listener— as "Hound Dog," "Tutti Frutti," "Who Do You Love?" or

"Johnny B. Goode." The most musically extreme record of Holly's time was Little Richard's "Ready Teddy": Elvis can't keep up with Little Richard, but Holly, despite guitar playing that almost rewrites the song from the inside out, can't keep up with Elvis.

Buddy Holly shied away from the violence implicit in rock 'n' roll as it first made itself known, and from the hell-fire emotionalism on the surface of the music. Performing under his own name or that of his band, the Crickets, he was a rockabilly original, but unlike Gene Vincent—or Carl Perkins, Jerry Lee Lewis, or the Sun label wild man Sonny Burgess, who after the release of his "Red Headed Woman" dyed his hair red and bought a red suit and a red Cadillac—Holly looked for space in the noise. He built his music around silences, pauses, a catch in the throat, a wink.

"That'll Be the Day" may be a very hard-nosed record, but its intensity is eased by its brightness, by the way it courts the prettiness that took over later Holly tunes like "Everyday," or even "Oh Boy" and "Rave On." "Hound Dog" aims for the monolithic and falls short; "That'll Be the Day" is a dozen ways of looking at life at once, and fully realized. The singer is acting out his role in different accents; like Rod Stewart combing his hair a thousand ways in "Every Picture Tells a Story," he's talking to the mirror, rehearsing what he's going to say, writing it down. He's saying it on the phone while the phone's still ringing at the other end, going over how perfectly he said what he meant to say after he's said it, or thinking of what he should have said after he's said what he didn't mean to say. Holly is reaching for Elvis's roughness, but even as he does so he communicates doubt that he can carry it off—or that anyone should. That's why "That'll Be the Day," a one-week number 1 hit in 1957, is a more convincing record than "Hound Dog," which with "Don't Be Cruel" on the flipside was an eleven-week number 1 hit in 1956—as Bobby Vee put it, thinking back to first hearing Holly on the radio in Fargo, North Dakota, when he was fourteen-year-old Bob Velline, "To me it was the most original, fresh, unique record I ever heard. And I was right, it was."

Holly could be sure of his self-doubt; Elvis couldn't be as sure of his arrogance, and so he muffles it with a self-mocking laugh: "As a great philosopher once said—" In that part of himself that was addressing "Hound Dog" to the world at large, to everyone who ever mocked him or the people he came from, you can hear Elvis meaning every word of "Hound Dog"; in the part of himself that was addressing the woman in the song, he's only kidding. Holly wasn't kidding on "That'll Be the Day." Holly's performance is tougher— just as "Well . . . All Right," a 1958 single with no orchestration other than acoustic guitar, string bass, and fluttered cymbals, a song inspired by the Crickets touring with Little Richard and hearing him shout "WELL ALRIGHT" at the slightest provocation, a performance that translated a Little Richard scream into a distant, simmering, quiet rebellion, is tougher still.

Holly's almost frightening sincerity was cut with playfulness, a risk-free sense of fun, and an embrace of an adolescent or even babyish innocence that was likely as calculated as his famous hiccups. Without that innocence and playfulness, his sincerity could have led him to take himself so seriously that today his music might sound hopelessly overblown; without his sincerity, many of his songs would now sound idiotic. Instead he so often struck a balance that was his alone.

"Anarchy had moved in," Nik Cohn wrote of the first days of rock 'n' roll. "For thirty years you couldn't possibly make it unless you were white, sleek, nicely spoken, and phony to your toenails—suddenly now you could be black, purple, moronic, delinquent, diseased, or almost anything on earth, and you could still clean up." What Buddy Holly was saying, what he was acting out, was that you could also be ordinary.

A photograph was taken in Lubbock, Texas, in 1955, on the occasion of Elvis Presley's second visit to Buddy Holly's hometown. In this picture, Elvis, at twenty, in a theater lobby or a crowded backstage, surrounded by teenage girls and boys and children, looks bigger than anyone else: taller, wider, taking up more psychic space. Even with his mouth hanging open, you can feel his glow. A month before, at his first show in Lubbock, "Elvis had signed girls' breasts, arms, foreheads, bras, and panties," the novelist Johnny Hughes wrote in 2009. "No one had ever seen anything like it."

Far behind him, just peeking into the frame, is an eighteen-year-old Buddy Holly, the only male figure, among thirty-odd people in the picture, wearing glasses, somewhere between geek and nerd, looking curious. He and two bandmates opened the show that day, supposedly Holly taught Elvis the Drifters' "Money Honey," but he holds no place in the crowd. You would never pick him out of the picture—or would you? No, probably not: there's no aura around his body, no portent in his posture, not even any obvious desire in his eyes. Just that curiosity: but even as he pokes his head forward for a closer look, he holds his body back. His curiosity is a form of hesitation, a drama of doubt. That quality of doubt is what gives the Buddy Holly in this picture the interest he has—and the longer you look at this picture, the less stable it appears to be. Who can identify with who? Who would want to identify with the nobody? But who can really identify with the god—and in this black-and-white photo, no matter the expression on his face, it's plain a god is in the room. Elvis Presley and Buddy Holly, sharing the same time and space: they're both magnets, Elvis the black hole, Holly merely earthly gravity.

It was Buddy Holly's embodiment of ordinariness that allowed him to leave behind not only a body of songs, but a personality—as his contemporaries Elvis, Chuck Berry, Little Richard, and Jerry Lee Lewis did, and Carl Perkins, Danny and the Juniors, Larry Williams, Fats Domino, the Monotones, Arlene Smith, and Clyde McPhatter did not.

The personality was that of the guy who you passed in the hall in your high school every day. He might be cool; he might be square. He might be the guy who slammed your locker shut every time you opened it, but the guy who did it as a laugh, a "Hey, man." He might be the guy who got his own locker slammed shut in his own face, and not in fun. Whoever he was, he was familiar. He was not strange; he was not different. He didn't speak in unknown tongues, or commune with secret spirits.

Except that he did. "Well . . . All Right" is not just a good song, or a startlingly modernist recording. With a quietness that like the silences in Robert Johnson's "Stones in My Passway" is also a form of loudness, the drum sticks moving across the cymbals like wind on water, the feel of death in the lack of any physical weight in the sound, the sense of a threat in every promise, "Well . . . All Right" is also the casting of a spell, but no one ever seemed less like a sorcerer than Buddy Holly.

"He was the patron saint of all the thousands of no-talent kids who ever tried to make a million dollars," Cohn said. "He was founder of a noble tradition." What Cohn is describing is how the gawky, wide-eyed Buddy Holly Gary

Busey summoned up for *The Buddy Holly Story* in 1978—someone who looks as if he's about to fall down every time he does the Buddy Holly move where he folds up his knees like a folding chair—is as believable as the cool, confident, hipster Buddy Holly that Marshall Crenshaw plays at the end of *La Bamba* in 1987, performing "Crying, Waiting, Hoping" on Holly's last stage, in Clear Lake, Iowa, then waving Ritchie Valens onto the plane: "Come on—the night belongs to the stars."

If Holly looked like an ordinary teenager, on the radio he came across as one, even if to the bookers at the Apollo Theater in New York, with no photos, only the radio to go on, he came across as black: after all, "That'll Be the Day" was a hit on R&B stations all across the country. His presence onstage, on the airwaves, seemed more accidental than willful. From his first professional recordings, the mostly dead-sounding numbers cut in Nashville in 1956, to the Clovis, New Mexico, sessions produced by Norman Petty in 1957, on through the soulful solo demos he made in New York in late 1958 and the beginning of the next year, the most glamorous element of Holly's career was the plane crash that ended it—on 3 February 1959, leaving his twenty-two-year-old body in an Iowa cornfield along with those of seventeen-year-old Ritchie Valens and twenty-nine-year-old J. P. Richardson, the Big Bopper, and the pilot, Roger Peterson, twenty-one.

So Buddy Holly entered history differently than other rock 'n' roll heroes—and his ordinariness carried over into the way in which one might encounter people whose lives brushed the end of his. Some years ago, on a panel in New Orleans, David Adler, author of the good book *The Life and Cuisine of Elvis Presley*, shocked me and everyone else in the room with the story of how, during his research in Tupelo, Mississippi, he met a woman who was in Vernon and Gladys Presley's one-room house when Elvis Presley was born —and he believed her, and we believed her, because of the way she described how the shoebox containing Elvis's still-born twin, Jesse Garon, was resting on the kitchen table.

A gasp went up. We were in the presence of someone who had been in the presence of someone who had been present when an event took place that ultimately would change the world—and leave all of us present in that world different than we would have otherwise been if this event had not taken place.

But nothing like that feeling attaches itself to the story I heard when, without asking, I found myself listening to a woman tell how, missing Buddy Holly's last concert as a twelve-year-old because no one she knew was vulgar enough to take her, she asked a friend to drive her to the site of the crash before the morning light was up, and how men with stretchers were still there when she arrived. Or listening to a woman who lived down the street from me in Berkeley describe how, as a girl, she witnessed the collision of two planes over Pacoima Junior High School, Ritchie Valens's alma mater, in 1957, a disaster that killed three students on the ground and, at least until he climbed onto a Beech Bonanza at the little airport in Mason City, Iowa, left Valens determined to stay out of the air if he could. Or listening in an Italian restaurant in New York in 1995 when, as if he'd never told the story before, Dion quietly went through the details of the life-threatening conditions he and everyone else endured while traveling the upper Midwest on ruined, heatless buses for the Winter Dance Party tour in January and February 1959 ("Dancing for teen-agers only," read the poster for the show at the Laramar Ballroom in Fort Dodge, Iowa, "Balcony reserved for adult spectators"), and why he nevertheless gave up his seat on the plane that night. Or listening in San Francisco in 1970, as Bobby Vee told the story of how, when the news of the plane crash reached Fargo Senior High School the next morning, with everyone geared up for the show that evening, just over the state line in Moorehead, Minnesota, Bob Veline and his high school band, which lacked a name and had not yet played a single show, answered the call of the local promoter and, after rushing out to buy matching sweaters and twenty-five-cent angora ties, and naming themselves the Shadows, took the stage that night—"For Buddy!"—along with those who were left.

Thus did Bobby Vee begin to tell his own part of the greater rock 'n' roll story, a story that—after he hired a young piano player in Fargo who was calling himself Elston Gunn and turned out to be a young Robert Zimmerman visiting from Hibbing, Minnesota; after Bob Veline became one of various post-Holly Bobbys, made over in terms of Holly's anybodyness, with anything that made this particular any-body unique airbrushed out—took the form of such first-rate teen-angst hits as "Take Good Care of My Baby" (number 1, 1961), "The Night Has a Thousand Eyes" (number 3, 1962), and, in 1962, *Bobby Vee Meets the Crickets*. The plane crash gave Bobby Vee his big break; as he saw it, it also gave him a legacy to honor, a mission to fulfill.

Because of the way Holly died—cut off in the bloom of youth, with his whole life ahead of him, chartering a plane because his clothes were filthy from the bus and he wanted to look good on stage, because he wanted to sleep for a few hours in a warm bed and do a good show—he immediately became a mythic figure. A queer mythic figure: a mythic figure you could imagine talking to. One you could ima-gine listening to what you had to say. As if, when John Len-non, Paul McCartney, and George Harrison, as the Quarry Men, cut a version of "That'll Be the Day" for their first recording, in Liverpool in 1958, and later named themselves the Beatles in imitation of Holly's Crickets, they were not simply copying a hero but conducting a kind of séance with him—just as the British rock 'n' roll producer Joe Meek, who would make his name in 1962 with the weird sound of the Tornadoes' "Telstar," actually did hold a séance in which, he said, he received the knowledge that Buddy Holly was going to die in a plane crash on February the third, just before his scheduled tour of the U.K. As Cathi Unsworth retells the true story in her murder mystery *Bad Penny Blues*, Joe Meek is James, and it's 1959:

> Toby frowned. "Oh," he said, not quite so amused now. "And when did he die again? It was early this year, wasn't it?"
>
> "Well, this is the thing," Lenny looked round at all of us. "They did the séance in January of '58, when Buddy was just about to come over. James sent him a message telling him not to get on a plane on that day, he was so convinced it was going to happen. But it didn't. Not that time anyway. It was exactly a year later when Buddy did get killed in a plane crash. February the 3rd, 1959."

It was Holly's ordinariness, his seeming approachability, that made this event an ineradicable figment of modern cultural memory. "Elvis Presley, Bo Diddley, Bill Haley & the Comets/were lies created on recording tape by the same Group/who made the Bomb, with the same motive: rule the world," the poet Charles Harper Webb wrote forty years after the fact. "Buddy Holly, Richie Valens, the Big Bopper died when their three/robots blew up in a thunderstorm."

"Your idea that I might take a plane/Through sleet and freezing rain/Is so vacuous," Paul Muldoon wrote in his song "It Won't Ring True" fourteen years after that. "Don't forget the whopper/Buddy told the Big Bopper/About getting off the bus." They are only two voices in a chorus that began singing the next day and will continue as long as there is anything in rock 'n' roll worth talking about.

But that sense of ordinariness, which led people to so readily attach their lives to Buddy Holly's, is also ridiculous. It's ridiculous that a full-length biography—Philip Norman's 1996 *Rave On*—could be written about someone who never reached the age of twenty-three, written without padding, without discographical pedanticism, quotidian minutiae, a potted social history of the 1950s, banal or for that matter profound musings on the emergence of the American teenager, rock 'n' roll, modern youth culture, or the meaning of the Alamo. And it's ridiculous that anyone could have left behind a body of work as rich as that Buddy Holly set down between the beginning of 1957 and the first weeks of 1959. But in that body of work—dozens of short, concise songs, most of them about two minutes long, some sharply shorter than that—is a story that can be told again and again without its ever being settled.

Many of the songs are obvious, despite a charm that isn't: "Everyday," "It Doesn't Matter Anymore," "Raining in My

Heart," "Heartbeat." "Even the obvious rockers, things like 'Rave On' or 'Oh Boy,'" Nik Cohn wrote, "were Neapolitan flowerpots after 'Tutti Frutti.'" Cohn was right. But more of what Holly did is unlikely before it is anything else.

You could start with "Not Fade Away," probably the oddest Buddy Holly record of all. On paper, it's nothing but an under-orchestrated Bo Diddley imitation. But as you hear it, no matter how many times you've heard it, it sounds nearly impossible. You can't date it by its sound, its style, the apparent recording technology. With Joe Mauldin on bass and Jerry Allison playing a cardboard box instead of drums, the music is all stop-time, every building theme cut off and brought up short, the whole song starting up again like the car it drops into the rhythm like a new dance step: "My love bigger than a Cadillac." With verbs evaporating out of the lyric, the song feels less like any kind of pop song than a folk song, and less like the Rolling Stones' 1964 wailing-down-the-highway version, their first American single, than the Beatles' "Love Me Do," their first single anywhere, from 1962, which the late Ralph J. Gleason, the music columnist for the *San Francisco Chronicle*, would refer to as "that Liverpool folk song," confusing some readers, like me, into wondering if perhaps it actually was.

The Rolling Stones heard the open spaces in "Not Fade Away," and what they did with it is a proof of how much room there was in Holly's songs. Mick Jagger had gone to see Buddy Holly and the Crickets at the Woolwich Granada theater in March 1958; supposedly they played "Not Fade Away." But while the Crickets start with a broken beat that could accompany someone doing the moonwalk on crutches, the Rolling Stones start with take-it-or-leave-it: an acoustic guitar strumming a pattern twice, hard, then a split-second of silence, then a single, isolated bass note, tipping the music into the air. And then it's a race, with Brian Jones's harmonica pulling ahead of the pulse that's pulling the music back, Bill Wyman's bass and Charlie Watts's drums watching the road while Keith Richards's guitar drives blind and Mick Jagger's voice says he's seen it all before. You go back to that first moment, that double pattern, that step off the cliff, trying to make the rest of the song match it.

You can hear the hit in the Rolling Stones' cover; the Crickets' original remains in another world. With the hesitations in the beat, in the singing, matched by the words fitted to them—"You drivin' me back"—the record isn't easy to listen to, because it doesn't quite make sense. Reaching at once for modernist abstraction and the symbolism of archaic ballads in which everybody dies, it speaks a defiantly absurdist language in the most modest, disappearing way. Always, when people have talked about the recordings Harry Smith brought to light on his anthology *American Folk Music*—the likes of William and Versey Smith's "When That Great Ship Went Down" from 1927, the Memphis Jug Band's "K. C.

Moan" from 1929, or Ken Maynard's "Lone Star Trail" from 1930—they've found themselves drawn to the same phrase. "This music sounds like it came out of the ground," people say, and that's what "Not Fade Away" sounds like—which is to say it also sounds more like flying saucers rock 'n' roll than Billy Lee Riley's "Flyin' Saucers Rock & Roll."

There is "Maybe Baby," a play on the Drifters' "Money Honey," except that here Clyde McPhatter's pratfalls are replaced by something close to a stalker's menace: not just words, "Maybe, baby, I'll have you," but the way Holly clips the last sound of each word, *MAY*be, *BAY*be, the slowness with which they're delivered, the slowness with which the words drag against the beat, which pulls against itself. The first hint of a personal aesthetic of drift, of floating, that would take over in Holly's apartment in New York the next year, is here in the ghostly backing vocals—it all seems to be happening in another dimension, where "maybe" is the ruling epistemological force, where nothing is certain and anything is possible. It's the same spot Holly found "Well . . . All Right," with its strange ellipsis, all but unknown in songtitling, where the drama is sealed at the end of each verse, the last word sliding into a dream the singer will dream for you if you won't dream it for him. It's the gentlest *fuck off*— to the world, to whoever might doubt a word he says, a fuck off that is also an extended hand.

There is "That'll Be the Day," written off of John Wayne's

ever-more-exasperated *"That'll* be the day" to Jeffrey Hunter across their five-year hunt for Natalie Wood in *The Searchers*. The Crickets first recorded it in Nashville for Decca in 1956; it was nothing, and the label shelved it along with everything else. The next year in Clovis they got it, the jangle of the guitar getting harder, sharper, with every note, and the band opening holes in the sound and then diving through them into some barely glimpsed other side, where they can look back at what they've already left behind. As if it had found and then become the template of all rock 'n' roll before it and all to follow, the performance generates its own momentum. It takes your breath away, that anything could be this simple, and this complete.

But "I'm Looking for Someone to Love," the flipside of the "That'll Be the Day" single, might be better. It begins as a thrill, a sound that seems huge because as with "That'll Be the Day" its internal rhythm is so strong. It's a sound that's also an enormous room, full of air, full of space, room for anything to happen, and almost everything does.

There are the backing singers, two men and two women, who swing as if they're on a swing, caught up in the fun, full of delight, real actors in this play, not props, every sound they make a shooting star of snapped-off cheerleader style. There's the lack of care in the singer's plea, the plea of someone looking for love, bereft, alone, but also cruising, not in any hurry, laughing at himself—and it's the lack of care that makes the room in the song, room in its story, in its heart, room, in this case, for the cool walk of the last verse, which turns out to be as complete a definition of rock 'n' roll as Holly's guitar solos, the verse that was nothing but a Holly family saying, which here seems a Zen koan, a frontier password, and lines left out of "Not Fade Away" all at once: "Drunk man / Street car / Foot slip / There you are."

Opening it up—as the first track on their first album, opening up the field of the Crickets' music itself, of their future—there's the lift, the crunch, and the release of what Holly does with his Fender Stratocaster. In "I'm Looking for Someone to Love," his solos are taken almost note for note from Roy Orbison's guitar solos on the B-side of his first single for the Sun label, "Go! Go! Go!"—but there's a difference. In "I'm Looking for Someone to Love" there's room in the song not only in terms of space and feeling, but in terms of time—there's time to do something other than what the song says you're supposed to be doing, that is, looking for someone to love. There's time to fool around, to get that sound that up until now you've only heard inside your head.

"Go! Go! Go!"—especially Orbison's solos and the rhythm behind him—is absolutely frantic. It's so fast that as Orbison sings the song he's also playing, he cannot keep up with himself. By the last verse he's actually gasping for breath—no metaphor, you can hear it. But Holly's solos, the same solos, have an elegance Orbison never thought of. As with

Bob Dylan's runaway-train harmonica solo in "Absolutely Sweet Marie," Orbison's signature is the bluegrass pause, a silence at just that instant when the music is at its highest —Wile E. Coyote as he realizes there's nothing beneath him but air, then the plunge down into what feels like an unthinkable increase in speed, in excitement, leaving the silence even more of a beckoning void than it was when the silence suspended the sound. That's Holly's signature too, here—but with a playfulness, a lack of fear, Butch Cassidy and the Sundance Kid losing ground to the Pinkertons behind them and knowing they'll get away somehow, one way or the other: "The fall'll probably kill you." A relaxing into speed, so that there's no way in the world, in this song, that Buddy Holly could fall behind himself.

There is "Peggy Sue," the number 3 hit from 1957, and the home recording, from 5 December 1958, of "Peggy Sue Got Married." Here is where the ordinariness the singer projects creates an intimacy with the listener—even though the quiet, troubled, happy man in "Peggy Sue Got Married" is hardly the hard, even avenging man in "Peggy Sue," a man who refuses to explain himself and demands that you believe him anyway.

This man rides the coldness of the music, as cold in "Peggy Sue" as the music in "Peggy Sue Got Married" is warm. There is the battering, monochromatic tom-tom rumble from Jerry Allison that opens "Peggy Sue," named for Allison's girlfriend, when the song was written: the next year Peggy Sue was Allison's wife, and eleven years after that his ex-wife. There is Joe Mauldin's bass strum behind that; there is the instrument beneath both that you barely register, Niki Sullivan's rhythm guitar. No leaps, no grand gestures, no gestures at all, just a head down into the wind the song itself is making, and then a harsh, cruel guitar solo, emerging as inevitably as any in the music, and also a shock. "If you knew, Peggy Sue"—the song is unexplainable, at least by me, but not by Jonathan Cott, writing in 1976.

"The women of Fifties rock 'n' roll, about whom songs were written and to whom they were addressed," Cott says, "were as interchangeable as hurricanes or spring showers, Party Doll ornaments of the song." But

> with Peggy Sue, Buddy Holly created the first rock and roll folk heroine (Chuck Berry's Johnny B. Goode is her male counterpart). And yet it is difficult to say how he did it. Unlike the Sad-Eyed Lady of the Lowlands—who Bob Dylan fills in as he invents and discovers her—Peggy Sue is hardly there at all. Most Fifties singers let it be known that they liked the way their women walked and talked; sometimes they even let on as to the color of their sweethearts' eyes and hair.
>
> But Buddy Holly didn't even give you this much information. Instead, he colluded with his listeners, suggesting that they imagine and create Peggy Sue *for him*. Singing in his characteristically shy, coy, ingenuous tone of voice,

Holly seems to let us in on a secret—just as later, in "Peggy Sue Got Married," he continues his complicit arrangement with his listeners, half-pleading with them, and with himself, not to reveal something which he himself must hesitatingly disclose. In this brilliantly constructed equivocation, Holly asks us to suspend disbelief . . . until that inexorable last stanza when we realize that no longer can Holly sing "You're the one" but only "She's the one." He has become one of his own listeners as Peggy Sue vanishes, like Humbert Humbert's Lolita, into the mythology of American Romance.

Buddy Holly "suggests" that his listeners "imagine and create Peggy Sue for him," Cott says. The idea sounds so unlikely, and yet in "Peggy Sue Got Married" it's literal: "I don't say / That it's true / I'll just leave that up to you."

And there are, finally, the remainder of Holly's last recordings, the solo pieces with guitar, acoustic or electric, that he taped in his and his new wife Maria Elena's apartment in Greenwich Village—though the word *finally* seems wrong, because these are also the recordings most suggestive of the music Holly had yet to make, and the life he had yet to live. There is a version of Mickey and Sylvia's "Love Is Strange" that is more than anything strange—so abstract, so much an idea of an idea, that the strings added after Holly's death let you imagine the singer resisting them in advance. Even odder, and far more affecting, is a reworking of Mickey and Sylvia's "(Ummm, Oh Yeah) Dearest" that is most of all a whisper—and, here, pure Holly, taken very slowly, as if the feeling the song calls up is so transporting that it would be a crime to let the song end. There is Holly's own "Learning the Game," sung with tremendous confidence, the singer moving right into the music, into the fatalism of the theme, riding the clipped guitar strum, no hesitation, no lingering —no speed, but no pauses, either. He never raises his tone, never increases the pressure.

And there is "Crying, Waiting, Hoping," from December 14, again an embrace of fatalism, but a step past anything he's done before. You can feel the great weight Holly gives the title words as the song begins. He follows a melody almost too sweet to bear, a melody hiding ghosts of countless other tunes, from a neighbor's "Shenandoah" when Holly was five to Johnny Cash's "I Still Miss Someone," playing on the radio as Holly sang into his tape recorder that December; as the melody turns toward the singer, then away from him, he tries to understand how each of the three words works as life. At the end he repeats the words again, isolating them from the rest of the song, and each from the other. They are a manifesto, a flag he's unfurling. "Crying—Waiting—Hoping"—the end.

It's this music that allows anyone to picture Buddy Holly in the years to come: to imagine his style deepening, his range increasing, his music taking shapes no one, not Holly, not his fans, could have predicted. When he died, Holly had plans for his own label, production company, publishing firm, management company, all under the name Prism; the business cards were printed, and a session with Waylon Jennings for Prism Records had already been produced. Holly saw himself recording with Ray Charles, or making a gospel album with Mahalia Jackson. He was spending time in Village jazz clubs and coffeehouses, at the Village Vanguard, the Blue Note, the Bitter End, Café Bizarre; he'd registered at the Actors Studio. But his career was slipping in late 1958, and his life was squeezed. He and the Crickets had split up. The money he'd made, a fortune, was sitting in a bank in Clovis, New Mexico, and sitting on that money was his producer and publisher Norman Petty, forcing him to live off loans from his wife's aunt, and finally to headline a tour in the upper Midwest in the dead of winter to make the rent and keep the idea of his own company alive. If you can see Buddy Holly as an entrepreneur in the music business, president of Prism Music, you can also see him, a year or two down the line, as a contract songwriter, side by side with the likes of Carole King, Gerry Goffin, Cynthia Weil, Barry Mann, Ellie Greenwich, and Jeff Barry at Don Kirshner's Aldon Music, at 1650 Broadway, Kirshner's Brill Building adjunct, Buddy Holly like everyone else writing songs for Bobby Vee. You can see him a year or two after that, Buddy Holly too wondering about the person everyone in the Village seemed to be talking about, and perhaps Holly, unlike the others, venturing out to see for himself.

As songwriters, Carole King and Gerry Goffin found levels of warmth and longing, hesitation and release, seduction and embrace, that escaped their peers. As recorded by the Chiffons, the Shirelles, and the Drifters, "One Fine Day," "Will You Love Me Tomorrow," and "Up on the Roof" are works of art. But there is no overstating how terrified the people at Aldon Music were of Bob Dylan and "Blowin' in the Wind."

"Unlike most of the songs nowadays being written uptown in Tin Pan Alley," Dylan would say in 1963, at the start of his "Bob Dylan's Blues," "that's where most of the folk songs come from nowadays, this wasn't written up there— this was written somewhere down in the . . . *United States.*" *You're fakes,* heard Goffin and King, nightclub prince Bobby Darin, Dion, and so many others: *You're fakes, and this is real.* In 2001, for a documentary on the Brill Building, Goffin spoke in broken, coulda-been-a-contender cadences, sounding used up, passed by: "I wish we had tried some songs that—really meant something . . . Dylan managed to do something that not one of us was able to: put poetry in with rock 'n' roll, and just stand up there like a mensch and sing it. And Carole felt the same way too, and so we had to do something dramatic, so we took all the [demos of] songs that hadn't been placed, not the songs there had been records on, and smashed them in half. We said, we gotta grow up, we gotta start writing better songs now." "There was a cultural phenomenon around us that had nothing to do with songwriting," King said on the same show, sitting around a table with Goffin, Weil, and Mann, a hint of contempt for the rest of them in her voice. "So it was: *Wait a minute! What's happening, what's going on? Things are changing. How do we write this stuff? Where do we fit in?*"

Buddy Holly might have been asking himself the same questions—or he might have already known the answers, might have already begun to live them out. If you can see Buddy Holly in his cubicle at Aldon Music, you can also glimpse the whole country of songs that, if he'd made his way only a few more years into the future, would have begun to gather around his. You can see him in the audience at Gerde's Folk City in 1960, perhaps there to catch the Texas folk singer Carolyn Hester: in 1957 he'd backed her on guitar in Norman Petty's studio in Clovis on his own "Take Your Time" and other tunes. He'd heard her sing the ancient "Black Is the Color (Of My True Love's Hair)"; when he and the Crickets played a movie theater in London, the show began with a ghostly organ sound, but no organ, no musician; then a platform rose from beneath the stage, revealing Holly alone at the keyboard, playing "Black Is the Color" as if it was the only song anyone needed to hear.

You might have found him in the backroom at the Gaslight Café, trading gossip with the folk-scene insider Fred Neil, a one-time pop singer and songwriter—Holly had recorded his "Come Back Baby" in 1958—or telling hometown stories with the Oklahoma blues and jazz singer Karen Dalton. You can spot him a year or so later, maybe at the Café Wha? watching Bob Dylan, who himself backed Carolyn Hester on harmonica for her third album, on, as it happened, a different "Come Back Baby," which she'd remember as an old blues he taught her, now getting up to sing "The Cuckoo" or "Moonshiner."

And you can see Bob Dylan back in the crowd not long after, watching as Holly, who Dylan would have noticed the minute he walked in, himself stood up to play "Not Fade Away," stamping his foot for the rhythm, or "Well . . . All Right," Dylan watching the smile on Holly's face for the "Well all right so I'm going steady/It's all right when people say/That these foolish kids can't be ready/For the love that comes their way" lines, Holly daring the hip crowd to laugh and no one laughing, everyone frozen by the way Holly let "the love that comes their way" drift into the haze of its own air.

It would have all come back to Bob Dylan, making notes that day on how Buddy Holly had somehow changed "Crying, Waiting, Hoping" into a blues, dropping the last word from a line and letting his guitar fill in the space with an invisible slide on the strings, that on 31 January 1959, he was present in the Duluth Armory for Buddy Holly's second-to-last show. He would have remembered that, as he would declare to the nation and the world when in 1998 he accepted the Grammy for Album of the Year for *Time Out of Mind*, "Buddy Holly looked right at me"—meaning that, on that night, Buddy Holly had passed on the secret of rock 'n' roll, of all music, of life itself, one avatar to another: a secret which, as of that night at the Grammys, Bob Dylan was plainly unready to pass on in turn.

Buddy Holly had not been dead for six months before his label, Coral, a subsidiary of Decca, got its hands on those last home recordings and brought in a staff producer to turn them into at least facsimiles of pop songs. The single "Peggy Sue Got Married" / "Crying, Waiting, Hoping" was released in September; passing unnoticed in the U.S., in the U.K. it was a hit. Just months away from the start of two years' work in the Augean stables of the Hamburg dives that would turn them into as tough a bar band as any in the world, playing five sets a night to drunken sailors, brawling locals, and hookers cruising the toilets, using every song they knew to make it to the next day, the Beatles played the record over and over, as if it were itself the séance Joe Meek had performed two years before.

With Holly's voice blown up far beyond the position it held in his real records, the overlay of piano, bass, guitar, and the Ray Charles Singers—a radio and TV chorus led by a Ray Charles who as a music-business professional went back to the thirties—was almost believable. At least it was for "Crying, Waiting, Hoping"—in "Peggy Sue Got Married," the way the backing singers answered Holly's "understand" with "*under-staah-haah-hand*" made Holly sound as dead as he was. For "Crying, Waiting, Hoping," there was a skittering, unpredictable guitar solo, as if a real person, someone who was working out the song with its composer, was part of the job. Most of all, the melody—in its essentials, the same melody Holly found for "Peggy Sue Got Married," the songs going into his tape recorder nine days apart—came through, and in both songs it was the melody that carried what the songs had to say, what they were trying to put into the world. It would have done so if Holly had recorded the songs without any words at all—the most modern attempts at "Crying, Waiting, Hoping," bitter, head-down performances by Keith Richards in 1993 and Cat Power in 2007, in both cases the pace slowed and the melody flattened, only highlight how strong, how resistant to any other element a performer might bring to it, the melody really is.

The melody describes innocence betrayed. Both the innocence and the betrayal are somehow embodied whole, but the power of the statement comes from the way they combine with each other, the innocence bright and sweet, the betrayal dank and full of rot, the innocent's shock at the first betrayal, the cold eye the betrayer casts back at the innocent, the innocent now seeing through the eyes of the betrayer, seeing himself, seeing herself. That was the engine of the song, and it was why the song never let go of those who tried to play it.

When Brian Epstein brought the Beatles, still with their drummer Pete Best, to Decca Records in London for an audition, "Crying, Waiting, Hoping" was one of the demos they recorded. The Beatles had everything riding on the session, which led to their rejection; so did Epstein. "Who can say with certainty that I was not born with a disability unfit for society to tolerate?" he once wrote in his diary; in 1956 in London he had been solicited by an undercover policeman, at first responded to and then rejected his entreaties, and was arrested for "persistently importuning." Homosexuality was still illegal; as a Jew who was ten years old when British soldiers liberated Bergen-Belsen and opened a new book of evil for all to read, a Jew whose rabbi was cursed and chased on the streets of Liverpool, Epstein knew himself as an outcast among those with whom he had been first cast out. By the mere facts of his life he was doubly a criminal—and this ugly fact too is part of where the Beatles came from, one of the motives behind their charm and their conquest.

"I was determined to go through the horror of this world," Epstein wrote in 1956, knowing nothing of his future. If his story is that "of an individual who had a hand in changing the world," as Debbie Geller wrote in 2000, then Epstein was a man who had to change the world to find a place in it. He had to make it bigger, wider, more open, less fixed and certain: along with the Beatles' pledge "To the toppermost of the poppermost," that was what was riding on "Crying, Waiting, Hoping" as the Beatles played it on New Year's Day, 1962. So famously, nothing came of the audition, at least not with Decca—a publishing executive at EMI, the most powerful and prestigious music company in Britain, heard something in Epstein's demos that Decca didn't and pulled strings to get the Parlophone producer George Martin to sign the group—as, less famously, nothing came of the Beatles' stab at Buddy Holly's song. George Harrison sang a stiff lead, and did a nice copy of the overdubbed guitar solo, but it was a second-class imitation of a record that was only half-alive to begin with. Still—is it an accident, or serendipity, that the Beatles escaped the same label that almost sank Buddy Holly? In 1957 Holly and the Crickets had re-recorded "That'll Be the Day" for Norman Petty in his Clovis studio. It was everything the 1956 Decca version, which the label had no intention of releasing, wasn't; they had to put it out. Holly called Decca to make sure the rights were clear, only to be told by the A&R man Paul Cohen ("The worst no-talent I ever worked with," he once said of Holly) that under no circumstances would Decca permit him to record any song he'd already recorded for them. For five minutes Holly is polite, probing, and calm as Cohen all but blows cigar smoke at him through the line, which Holly had hooked up to his tape recorder. Ignoring Decca, Petty sold the new record to the Brunswick label; Decca was about to sue when it realized it already owned Brunswick, and would thus be suing itself.

A year and a half later, in the midst of a year in which the Beatles' first and second albums, *Please Please Me* and *With the Beatles*, would occupy the number 1 position in the British charts for fifty-two consecutive weeks—and no one would have believed, even at the end of that year, that this was only a harbinger of things to come—a new confidence, bravado, arrogance, assurance should have gone into the song. But while at a show in London the Shirelles' "Baby It's You" brought out everything the group had to give, two weeks later in the same hall "Crying, Waiting, Hoping" brought out nothing. With dull strummed backing and tuning straight from the Shadows, the instrumental group that had dominated the British charts for years, it was boilerplate Merseybeat. Without a musical dimension, there was nothing to hear but words, and with the roar of novelty at the heart of Beatlemania, a new world sighted if not yet reached, the song sounded old.

Four years later, it could seem as if the Beatles had done more than change the world. It could seem as if they owned it, or as if they were it, as if every voice on earth went into theirs and was sent back to whoever it came from with more vitality, more intelligence, more heart, and more love, leaving not only the world, but individual girls and boys, men and women, changed. And still there was no end to the sense of surprise that was the truest source of the change the Beatles had made.

No one had ever heard anything like it; no one has heard anything like it since. That is the first thing to remember about "A Day in the Life," the last track on the Beatles' *Sgt. Pepper's Lonely Hearts Club Band,* an album that, at least in its moment, made almost every other performer in rock 'n' roll feel incomplete, inarticulate, fraudulent, and small: left behind.

As 1966 broke into 1967, it was a time in rock 'n' roll—in life lived according to its pace—when no one knew what to expect. Album by album, the Beatles, Bob Dylan, the Rolling Stones, even the Beach Boys, even someone who might not have been heard of the year or the month before, were in a constant battle to top each other. On 29 August 1966, in San Francisco, the Beatles had played what would turn out to be their last show, an event that, in its absence, would transform the group. George was spending time in a London ashram, days that would transform his life. On a night that would transform his, John Lennon had met the conceptual artist Yoko Ono. Still, no one, perhaps not even the Beatles themselves, were ready for the daring of "A Day in the Life"—for its bet that the future had already arrived.

It was the second song to be recorded for *Sgt. Pepper,*

made in January and February of 1967, but in a way it wasn't part of the album at all. *Sgt. Pepper* was constructed as a music-hall review, harking back to the 1920s or even before. It began and ended with the title celebration and its reprise, with rousing shouts from the stage and deliriously happy applause from the crowd. Then, creeping out of the last burst of affirmation as it faded back into the past—"A 'regular' movie," Pauline Kael once wrote, "says yes to the whole world or it says not much of anything," and that's what "Sgt. Pepper's Lonely Hearts Club Band" said—the present, in the form of its wars, greed, vanity, and triviality, returned.

That determined, bright strum from John's acoustic guitar, placing the listener right on the steps to the door that was about to open; the loose, floating notes from Paul's piano, disconnected, abstract, distracting you from the feeling that something was about to happen, making you forget why you were waiting for the door to open—it was like a play, complete and finished in a few seconds.

John had written three verses about reading the news: a car crash and a movie opening in London, a count of pot-holes in "Blackburn, Lancashire" somehow matching the number of seats in the Albert Hall. DJs quickly told their listeners that the person who "blew his mind out in a car" in the first verse was Tara Browne, a Beatle hanger-on and heir to the Guinness fortune who was killed in an auto accident, and that the film the singer saw in the second verse was *How*

I Won the War, starring John himself, who died at the end, but none of that mattered. It wasn't only the notes in the song that floated; it was the play itself. The story unfolded like a dream, dissolving each time you tried to make its details into facts.

But it was too much of a dream. The story was pierced by a piece of song that Paul McCartney had been holding onto, an account of a commuter rushing for the bus, and this was the prosaic anchor the song needed. The commuter makes the bus, goes upstairs for a smoke, and drifts off— returning, as Devin McKinney wrote in 2003, to "the dream from which he believed he had been awakened." And there is "a sound building up from nothing to the end of the world," as John put it when he demanded an orchestra to take the song into a maelstrom. "We'll tell the orchestra to start on whatever the lowest note on their instrument is," Paul remembered saying to John, "and to arrive at the highest note on their instrument, but to do it in their own time." In their own time—that was the source of the danger in the heart-stopping climb that took the everyday to the face of eternity. There were random cymbal slashes from Ringo Starr broken up in the noise; a stentorian, counting voice disappearing into the whirlwind, and then a single, giant chord, three pianos struck at once, then a slipping, droning forty-three seconds from a thunderclap to a buzz that never quite reached silence.

Page upon page has been written on the song as a poem of alienation, an echoing damn on all the works of modern life. In 1984, Jon Wiener noted that while the *Sgt. Pepper* song-cycle ends with the band thanking its "lovely audience," "A Day in the Life" ends with the audience described as empty holes, and perhaps this explains anything that needs to be said about what the song means. Very little has been said about the way the song's meaning is conveyed. The song created an altogether new field of expression, one that was never occupied again; the question of how that field was made remains open.

As the song begins, both John's singing and the melody he is tracing are intentionally following in the tracks of Elvis Presley's 1956 "Heartbreak Hotel." Then the song leaps forward, past itself, past 1967, and past the Beatles, to the last moments in John's 1970 "God," the last song on his first solo album, where, in the absurdly pompous line, "I was the dreamweaver," he found the most sublime singing of his life and of his time; it was the way he put his whole being into "was." "A crowd of people turned away," he sings of the movie he goes to see in "A Day in the Life," his tone echoing that moment three years later in advance, in the quiet sweep as he lets the words drift, so that you can picture the crowd as a wave, a single body and no mind. "But I just had to look—"

"You never use the word 'just,'" John once said. "It's meaningless. It's a fill-in word." In the handwritten lyrics for Lennon's part of "A Day in the Life," you can see where he omitted the word in the line that follows "I just had to look": "Just having read the book." There it is, the fill-in word. But in the previous line—"I just had to look"—*just* can mean nothing, or it can be an absolute. *I had to look, I had no choice*—here "just" pulls down against the other words, making its own music, allowing the "had" to rise up like a spirit, making you feel you would give anything to follow it.

"A Day in the Life" remains a play in which the most casual events of the day, the stories in the paper, anyone's morning routine, turn into inexplicable threats. Daily life becomes a circus, at just that point where someone cuts the ropes holding up the tent. As cheers ride the band off the stage, as the boards pile high with bouquets thrown from all over the theater, even the balconies, a figure dressed in white tie and tails stands in the wings. He looks out into the crowd, where even strangers are embracing, and as the last round of applause drops away he steps forward. He is there to bring the news that, outside the theater, nothing has changed. The hall falls silent. As the members of the audience leave the building, they become the crowds that will course through "A Day in the Life," averting their eyes from the smashed car in the street outside, walking briskly past the headlines on the hoardings, trying to get the sound of the man's voice out of their heads.

CRYING, WAITING, HOPING

That was the high point of the Beatles' career. Three months after the release of *Sgt. Pepper* Brian Epstein died in London of a drug overdose, likely a suicide. After that the Beatles stumbled, for a moment finding their footing in 1968 with the collection of disparate sessions that produced what came to be known as "the White Album"—where, Jann Wenner wrote at the time, "It's possible that they are no longer the Beatles." At the beginning of the next year they went into the studio, with Yoko Ono sitting at John's side as the last in a long line of Fifth Beatles, for a recording marathon they were calling "Get Back"—a return to roots for a band whose history so matched that of rock 'n' roll itself that they were their roots. There was backbiting and insult, dismissal and the deadly expressions that didn't need words. George and Ringo quit the band and then returned and quit again. Paul tried to keep one day following another. John was there but already gone.

They had all the money in the world, and time was running out. They went into the studio day after day and came out with nothing. They tried the first songs John and Paul had ever written together, the first songs they'd played. They even went back to "That'll Be the Day," and got no farther with it than they had eleven long years before, in another world. Then one day, at the end of January, for a few minutes another country, that country of songs, came into view.

There's a flurry of rhythm, some random tuning up, then

a harsh stop. Then a guitar note that fills in the silence, then drums, then George slashing chords out of the shimmering tones of a guitar run through a Leslie box, lining out "Not Fade Away," John shouting words from far back in the sound, then adding organ. At first the borrowed Bo Diddley beat is all they have: John sings a line from Dee Clark's Diddley knockoff "Hey Little Girl," then a line from Bo Diddley's "Bo Diddley." Everyone but George seems to lose interest—the abstraction at the heart of the song is leaving them mute and handless—but they press on, as if they can't think of anything better to do. Then on a cue from John there's a tip into "Maybe Baby," and a hint of the band driving its own car, the song merely the gas, and the tune almost takes on a body. It's full, strong—and it begins to come apart in an instrumental break. John comes back, earnest, still reaching for the song, and then without a pause, by some trick of the light, "Maybe Baby" is replaced by "Peggy Sue Got Married." It's hot, sharp, the words scrambled back into "A Day in the Life"—"Peggy read the news the other day"—George searching for a spine in the song, letting the melody carry him, then realizing the melody is the spine. Singing "Winkin' and blinkin' and nod," bits and pieces of God knows what, "You say you care, you're everywhere," John begins to do what people have always done with fifties songs, mock them, turn them into jokes to mock one's own helpless affection for them, but it doesn't work; the mockery doesn't work, and then neither does the song. They hit a wall—the wall dividing their love for the music they can no longer play from whatever music they might still have ahead of them. And then there's a high, metallic half-phrase from a rhythm guitar, everyone knowing what it is, where it's from, what it's for.

"Crying, Waiting, Hoping": they dance around the sound that's still hanging in the air, knowing this is where it will happen or fail. "We used to do it," someone says sadly, defeat all over his voice. "It ended with, ah—" George says. John plays a fragment of a chorus on his guitar. The words begin to come to him like birds. The singing is ragged, but they're all part of it, with John's fragmented lead only a step ahead of anyone else. *Hopin' you'll come back*—and then a flood of emotion into a single syllable that expands to fill the whole room and sharpens like a drill to drive down into the ground beneath it: *"Mine."* All you hear is heart and melody—the heart the melody was crafted to bring out.

The song gives them freedom: they're lost in it, they're home. Structure doesn't matter, the right words have no meaning, the progression of going where you're supposed to go dissolves into the paradise of finding that you've arrived without will or even wish in the place you want to be. There's something in the dynamics of the song, in the switchbacks of the melody, that demand that anyone who has truly found the song rewrite it on the spot—live it out.

CRYING, WAITING, HOPING

"Smokin'," says Paul. "Jokin'," John answers. Time and again John returns to "Hopin'—you'll come back"—and as you hear the group coming apart across these sessions, the bell rings all too clearly. They love this song, and they love each other, or they remember that they did. It's heartbreaking, and it's nothing to what's coming.

At the right moment, George moves into the mandated solo, that grave-robber's overdub he learned ten years before. "You'll come back," Paul sings, high, keening, over George's first notes, as if the line got away from him, the words unbidden. George plays the same formal passage he played in 1962 and 1963, but everything is different. John and Paul are talking, singing, in the background; there is no separation, every sound is part of every other. Everyone shares in the laughter, the embarrassment at how much the song is asking of them and how much, now, at the end, they have to give it.

George's notes are liquid, unstable, shifting into each other, a swirl of clothes, jackets and ties and shirts and scarves floating by like pages blown off a calendar by the wind of an old movie. More emotion flies out with each measure. The Leslie effect allows every note to melt, matching the singing. It's a crude, broken mess of such beauty it makes no sense. The notes begin to turn over; the song is doing cartwheels. As George picks his way through the memory of the song—the memories the song sparks of when they used to do it, when they tried to nail what attracted them to it in the first place, but also what the song itself remembers, the years it has traveled, the bodies it has inhabited, the voices that have tried and will try to speak its language—the whole history of the Beatles is present, as loss. And suddenly, that's all you hear. Everything they ever had shines more brightly as, here, they feel its absence, feel what has slipped away, what can never be recaptured. Once they sent an idea of friendship out all over the world: the idea of a group that could bring out the uniqueness of the individual more completely than he or she could ever do alone. Now they are putting that into the world one last time, but secretly, in a broken performance they have no reason to think anyone will ever hear.

It's painful—but not as painful as the way John pulls the song to an end and freezes the music, dismissing the loose joy of what has just transpired by shifting into one more Buddy Holly number, "Mailman Bring Me No More Blues." What he has just done is painful to him; he doesn't want to think about what he can never have again. It's better to pretend that liberty never existed at all, so he closes the rhythm like a lock. A dead cadence overrules anything else anyone might bring to the music. The song counts the steps down the stairs and out of the building, leaving all of the freedom they'd stumbled upon behind, and good riddance.

With their melodies intertwined, "Crying, Waiting, Hoping" always circled back to "Peggy Sue Got Married"; together they made a Möbius strip. A "rock 'n' roll folk heroine," Jonathan Cott called Peggy Sue; he meant that like Handsome Molly or Pretty Polly or Omie Wise or Barbara Allen, the folk heroines Bob Dylan sang about in the Gaslight in 1962, Peggy Sue too had entered the language, floated free in cultural space and time. She "continued to live on," Cott wrote, "making an appearance not only at the living room party" in Bobby Darin's "'Splish Splash' but also in" his "'Queen of the Hop' and Ritchie Valens's 'Ooh My Head' — finally to be scorned and discarded for a younger rival in the insolent 'Barbara Ann': 'Played our favorite tune/Danced with Betty Lou/Tried Peggy Sue and I knew she wouldn't do—'"

Cott even finds Peggy Sue in the first two letters of the Beatles' "P.S. I Love You" — but the real story of how Peggy Sue lived on is closer to the tale Buddy Holly told, and acted out, throughout his career.

Before "Peggy Sue" was a song, Peggy Sue Gerron left Lubbock Senior High, where she'd first met Buddy Holly — rushing to make an assembly where he was to perform, he knocked her over, apologizing for not having time to help her up, but taking the time to tell her she had pretty lips — for Sacramento, California, finishing high school at Bishop Armstrong Catholic Girls School. In James Marsh's 1993 documentary film *Peggy Sue* — a biography, as Marsh conceived it, of the song, not the person — Peggy Sue Rackham, by then co-owner of the Sacramento sewer and drainage repair company Rapid Rooter, describes going to see the Crickets in 1957 at the Sacramento Memorial Auditorium, and hearing herself coming off the stage. In Marsh's film there is fabulous silent color footage of the band, not in perfect focus but carrying excitement, pride, triumph, the band in handsome dark suits, Holly on his knees, Joe Mauldin on his back, Jerry Allison moving behind his drum kit as if he's spinning in circles—but as Peggy Sue tells the story, she doesn't sound altogether happy. She is not a woman who smiles.

In her early fifties, Peggy Sue looks her age as anyone would want to. Dressed in a black-and-white striped blouse and pants, she is a trim woman with short blonde hair—the same haircut she had in high school. From about 1957, there's a picture of her in a cheerleader costume, her legs splayed out on the school grass in a shockingly seductive pose. And then we see another woman, thickset, with a blonde brush-cut: a Sacramento businesswoman named Donna Fox. There's a picture of her at fifteen, when she was Donna Ludwig: she's so pretty she makes you blink. Ritchie Valens's "Donna" plays on the soundtrack. He had sung it for her over the phone, but she had no idea it was a record until she heard it on the radio, cruising the strip with her girlfriends, and they all began to scream. "It was wonderful," she says thirty-five years later, all heart.

"I never knew there was a Peggy Sue," Fox says in the film; Peggy Sue didn't know there was a Donna. "And it was even more amazing," Rackham says, "to find out we were living in the same town—and had for years. I called Donna at her office, and luckily got her on the phone. 'Is this Ritchie Valens' 'Donna'?' 'Yessssss . . .'" Rackham remembers Fox saying, her guard up—she'd had calls like this before. "'Well—this is Buddy Holly's Peggy Sue.'

"'Want to do lunch?'"

The film ends with a TV commercial for Rapid Rooter: workmen repair a broken line, fix a pipe. "Oh, yes, I've used Rapid Rooter many times," Donna says from behind her desk. "Last time, my drain was clogged, and by the time I got out of the shower and blew my hair dry, there was a note on my door, thanking me for my business. I've recommended it to all my friends." Then Peggy Sue, standing next to a Rapid Rooter van: "When there's a plumbing problem," she says, "we're here for you."

Peggy Sue Rackham and Donna Fox were appearing as themselves, both ordinary and immortal. That someone could be both was, really, the Buddy Holly story; the story Buddy Holly had just time enough to tell.

Instrumental Break

Another History of Rock 'n' Roll

On 21 February 2012, at the end of a White House blues night, President Obama sang a chorus of Robert Johnson's "Sweet Home Chicago." Two weeks later, to mark Johnson's centennial—likely a year late, not that anyone cared—the Apollo Theater in New York staged the tribute concert "Robert Johnson at 100," featuring, among many others, the Roots, offering "Milkcow's Calf Blues," Living Colour with "Preachin' Blues," Elvis Costello with "From Four Until Late," both James Blood Ulmer and Taj Mahal in turn with "Hell Hound on My Trail," Bettye LaVette with "I'm a Steady Rollin' Man" and "When You Got a Good Friend," Macy Gray with "Come on in My Kitchen," Shemekia Copeland with "Stop Breakin' Down Blues," and Sam Moore with "Sweet Home Chicago." It's hard to imagine that had Robert Johnson lived any longer than he actually did, or lived a different life, he would have ever gained greater renown or respect, or that his music would have traveled any farther than it has.

Listening to the records Johnson made in the 1930s, you may find yourself entering the world of an African-American in his mid-twenties, from Mississippi, in an area centered around Clarksdale, in the midst of the Great Depression, with that distant, closed place, where blacks worked on plantations or in the peonage of the tenant farm system, and were not allowed to vote, serve on juries, or fulfill any of the civil rights of an American citizen, rendered in a handful of compositions falling into the already defined school of what would later be called Delta blues. At the same time, you will find yourself in a world where no geographical or period definition holds and no social or stylistic boundaries are fixed: in a confusion of desire and terror, satisfaction and defeat, that has always marked men and women and their deepest art. What you hear may seem impossibly far away, with unfamiliar place names and archaic phrases, and the emotional impact may be instant, the sound of love and hate, affection and estrangement, fatalism and nihilism, life and death. And yet this music was almost lost.

When Columbia issued the first collection of Johnson's recordings, in 1961, he was all but unknown outside of small circles of such Mississippi-born Chicago bluesmen as Muddy Waters and equally small circles of fiercely cultish blues record collectors, and that made the title the album carried—*King of the Delta Blues Singers*—go off like a bomb. The idea of some forgotten nobody ruling over a kingdom of music as deep as the Mississippi—what was this, the Man in the Iron Mask? "I immediately differentiated him from anyone else I had ever heard," Bob Dylan later wrote of hearing a prerelease copy of the album he was given by his new Columbia producer, John Hammond. Dylan had never heard of Johnson; neither had his Greenwich Village mentor Dave Van Ronk, who, it had seemed, knew everything there was to know about everything. Before long Johnson would be celebrated as the most influential of all blues artists. The likes of Taj Mahal's 1967 "The Celebrated Walking Blues," Cream's 1968 live version of "Crossroads," Led Zeppelin's 1969 performance of "Traveling Riverside Blues," and, from the same year, the Rolling Stones' increasingly dreamlike recordings of "Love in Vain," made Johnson's music common coin. More than forty years later, after scores if not hundreds of musicians had pursued the investigation of Johnson's twenty-nine recorded compositions as if they were detectives and the music was the crime, only the full fathom five of Cat Power's 2002 dive into "Come on in My Kitchen" was a surprise.

In 1986, Robert Johnson entered the Rock and Roll Hall of Fame as a member of its first class. That same year his "Cross Road Blues" sold Cross Road Beer; in 2000 it powered Toyota's "Crossroads of Value" campaign. By 1994, his face was on a U.S. postage stamp. Robert Johnson was a commodity. But despite the discovery of the facts of his life and even photographs—in 1961, when there were almost no facts and no known photographs, for the Johnson album cover Columbia made do with a painting of a man bent over his guitar, shown from the back—he remained a myth, the sort of figure Dylan could say "seemed like a guy who could have sprung from the head of Zeus."

The files showed that he had recorded in a San Antonio hotel room in 1936 and in a Dallas office building in 1937. Interviewed in the 1960s, blues players who had worked with Johnson, or said they had, told researchers he had been killed after a show at a juke joint near Three Forks, Mississippi. He had taken up with the club owner's wife and was given poisoned whiskey. It was said that he was found on his hands and knees, "barking like a dog." "Men and women are down on all fours growling and snapping their teeth and barking like dogs," the cultural critic Gilbert Seldes wrote in 1928, in *The Stammering Century*, a history of the American eighteen hundreds as a history of utopian cults and religious insanity, describing a camp-meeting revival in Kentucky around 1800—and you can imagine that the storied description of Johnson's death is less a literal account, or even a rumor, than a mandated cultural memory, a way of saying that when one plays with the devil, as Johnson did in "Me and the Devil Blues" and "Hell Hound on My Trail," this is how that person's fate must be described. The lack of facts magnified such stories; in the postwar imagination Johnson was a myth before he was a real person, and because of the character of his music, that is what he remains. "A dog, a dog," David Lynch wrote in 2001, in his song "Pink Western Range," "barking like Robert Johnson."

Legends, like snakes, began to wrap themselves around Johnson almost immediately after his death: tall tales, hints of the supernatural, of someone who could be in two places at once, of magic potions, of disguises and false names and impersonations, spring up straight from the kind of blues Johnson wrote and sang, the hoodoo tradition in which he staked a claim. The story that Johnson sold his soul to the devil first appeared in print in 1966, when the blues historian Pete Welding interviewed the Mississippi Delta bluesman Son House. House told Welding—as he had earlier told the blues promoter Dick Waterman, who in 1964 found House living in Rochester, New York, unknown and forgotten— that in the early '30s in Clarksdale, when House had records with his name on them, Johnson was a pest. "Man, he was always hanging around with me and Willie Brown, wanting to sit-in and do a song," Waterman remembered House say- ing. "We let him sit-in and he would up and break a string, and where we gonna get a new string late Saturday night, man? And we had to tie that broken string together and tear up our fingers! We didn't want *him* to play." R. Crumb once drew a picture of the milieu: as the older bluesmen Charley Patton and Willie Brown compose on a front porch, a lithe teenager, his eyes wary as they dart toward the two, passes by. Then Johnson went away. When he returned, a year later, maybe more—no one had missed him—he confronted the men who had driven him off with a propulsive rhythmic charge that was like a train they could never catch, a delicacy of technique they realized they could never master, and a treasure of feeling none of them would ever express. "He sold his soul to the devil in exchange for learning to play like that," House told Welding. But the notion of the blues singer selling his soul to the devil was a commonplace, and for that matter a selling point: "That word 'devil,'" the blues singer Henry Townsend once said. "You'd be surprised how *effective* it is." Tommy Johnson, from Jackson, Mississippi, whose late '20s recordings about women and alcohol—"Cool Drink of Water Blues," "Big Road Blues," "Canned Heat Blues," and more—made indelible marks on the body of American music, bragged about it, and even detailed how to do it. Howlin' Wolf did nothing to dissuade people from the rumors that he had made the pact—the fierceness of his sound and the anarchy of his performance seemed to confirm it. The story of Robert Johnson and the devil was circulating in New Orleans in the late 1940s; well before Son House told his tale, the Chicago guitarist Mike Bloomfield said in an interview in 1981, just before he was found dead of an overdose in his car in San Francisco, he had heard the story again and again from South Side blues players.

It was in the 1970s that the music scholars Mack McCormick and Steve LaVere, working independently, were able to track down Johnson's surviving half-sister in Baltimore and reconstruct his life. Unless they found the sister of another Mississippi blues singer with the same name, as some have claimed—Johnson went by several names—he was born on 8 May 1911, in Hazlehurst, Mississippi, in the southwest corner of the state. His childhood was a confusion of parents and stepfathers, spent first in labor camps, then in Memphis, then in Robinsonville, Mississippi, thirty miles south of Memphis, in the Delta, a place that was by 1915 the spawning ground of Mississippi blues, and a center of artistic inspiration hotter than anything the Surrealists would conjure up in Paris. As a boy, Johnson like anybody else fooled around with a diddley bow, a wire stretched on a length of wood or the side of a house. He played Jew's harp, then harmonica. But now he encountered the first recognized progenitors of the Delta blues: Patton, Brown, and House, musicians who would one day be named the founders of a tradition that underwrote all of modern popular music. It was a shibboleth, perfectly sent up in *All You Need Is Cash*, Eric Idle's appallingly perfect Beatles parody, where all of the music of the Fab Four is traced back to one Ruttling Orange Peel, telling his tale to an interviewer from the BBC as the Mississippi unwinds in the background ("They got it all from me")—a shibboleth of irresistible poetic force. "It was the first time in history," the singer Jack White said in 2013, as he prepared to reissue recordings by Patton and others, "that a single person was writing a song about themselves and speaking to the world by themselves." "Listen," the producer T Bone Burnett said the year before, "the story of the United States is this: One kid, without anything, walks out of his house, down the road, with nothing but a guitar and conquers the world." Jonathan Lethem made the case best of all: "Pop was a trick, a perverse revenge against the banality of daily life dreamed up collectively by ten or fifteen Delta bluesmen and a million or a hundred million screaming twelve-year-old girls."

On acoustic but sometimes uncannily resonant steel-bodied guitars, the Delta players made a loud, percussive music. A knife, or a bottle on a finger, drawn down the strings, matched and extended the timbre of the voice, so that a song would say what its words never could, and hint at the notion that some things couldn't be put into words, or shouldn't be. Inside the loudness was a music of almost infinite subtlety: a complex of style and emotion that brought out the individuality of the singer so forcefully that the drunk making noise in a juke joint could suddenly appear as a trickster or a prophet, placed in front of you to take what you had, or give you knowledge you didn't want, reveal truths about yourself you didn't want to hear.

On the radio, on phonographs or jukeboxes, Johnson listened to Son House's "Preachin' the Blues" and to Willie Brown's "Future Blues"—and to the smooth-voiced singer Lonnie Johnson, Jimmie Rodgers's blue yodels, and Skip

James's unearthly "Devil Got My Woman," just as in years to come he would take in Bing Crosby's "Brother, Can You Spare a Dime" and Leroy Carr's rolling piano reverie "When the Sun Goes Down." As an itinerant musician, often traveling with the guitarist Johnny Shines, he played whatever anyone called for. "Polka," Shines once said. "Irish. Jewish. Well, like 'Stardust.' 'Danny Boy.'" The records Johnson made, though few sold well even by local standards, made him a name. If at first he often performed with his back turned away from other musicians, near the end of his life he may have been playing with a pianist and a drummer, with ROBERT JOHNSON painted on the bass drum.

The story of his death—according to a death certificate discovered in 1968, he died on 16 August 1938—is, depending on how you want to look at it, romantic or squalid. It tells you tales you want to hear, even if it tells you nothing about why the music Robert Johnson left behind sounds like part of a tradition mostly in the sense that in it you can hear what all who preceded him in the blues tradition, and all who followed him, seemed to have been reaching for. It says nothing about why his songs can sound as if they came out of nowhere, as if for all he shared with his contemporaries, or even you or me—the English language, a suit and tie—he sang and played in a language that was his alone.

That sense of things is most obvious in an obviously dramatic song like "Cross Road Blues." The singer is faced with a terror he can't or won't name, let alone escape; the guitar is muscled and unyielding. But "Cross Road Blues" soon surrenders to songs where nothing is obvious. In other hands, "Dust My Broom" and "Sweet Home Chicago" are declarations of pride and adventure. What's so striking in Johnson's originals is the way, in the choruses, Johnson drops the bottom out of the tunes, suddenly replacing all that was optimistic and energetic—the fabulous Chicago grin of "I'm booked, and I gotta go!"—with fatigue and doubt. No matter how carefully fashioned, the music is never completely stable. You can feel the artifice in "Kind Hearted Woman Blues"; you can feel it burn off like fog as Johnson's voice goes up high and then all but disappears with "Oh, babe— my life don't feel the same," leaving the song as abandoned as the woman in the song has left the man. In "Traveling Riverside Blues," danger and risk, flight and hesitation, are foreshadowed in the opening guitar flourishes—but everything comes back harder, scarier, in a split second at the end, as if the fine story of sex and whiskey Johnson has told was a con, softening up the listener for a truth the singer can tell only by concealing it.

The ground comes out beneath your feet: you don't know where you are in Johnson's songs. You are in the somewhere they come from, the somewhere they go—and never more so than in "Come on in My Kitchen." There were two versions; in the recording that was originally released, in 1936, the music slips away from the song, the words miss each other like people walking in the dark. That was the second take. But with the first, which only saw the light of day in 1961, on *King of the Delta Blues Singers*, everything is in perfect balance—a balance so perfect you are aware that a single wrong breath could tumble it all to ruin. And that balance, as Bob Dylan once described the experience of writing "Like a Rolling Stone," would have been a matter of "a ghost is writing a song like that, it gives you the song and it goes away"—and when it's gone, it's gone.

In deathly quiet, a man sings to a woman; simply by opening his mouth he reveals their absolute isolation, each isolated from the other, both alone in the world. What a trance Johnson must have put himself into in that San Antonio hotel room to play and sing as he did on that day! Between each couplet, a void opens, and with impossibly evanescent high notes Johnson traces a bridge that isn't there. It's a cadence where beauty is married to dread; a movement slipping forward toward death, where every second counted off on the guitar is one more second used up in life. There's a sting at the end of the last note of the progression; like a snake's tail, the note curls back. Again, again, again: what these passages enact is forgiveness. Of the woman in the song, for needing to be saved. Of the man singing, because he can't save her. Of the world, for leaving both of them stranded, bereft, needing what they can't have.

INSTRUMENTAL BREAK

153

If Robert Johnson hadn't died when he did, on the same day Elvis Presley would die thirty-nine years later, he might very well have been part of John Hammond's "From Spirituals to Swing" concert at Carnegie Hall on 23 December 1938, along with the Count Basie Orchestra, Sister Rosetta Tharpe, Big Joe Turner, Mitchell's Christian Singers, Sonny Terry, Jimmy Rushing, and the Golden Gate Quartet. Hammond, who was stunned by Johnson's records, had scouts searching for him; when he learned that Johnson was dead, Hammond replaced the already-advertised Johnson with the blues singer Big Bill Broonzy, but still played his 78 of Johnson's "Walking Blues" from the stage.

If Johnson had been there in the flesh, he might have gone back to Mississippi; if so, there is no reason to think he would not have disappeared from public life as completely as Tommy Johnson, Skip James, Son House, and many more—artists who lived on in obscurity for decades after they wrote their names in invisible ink on the American map, unseen and unheard. If Johnson hadn't been killed, he might have settled in Chicago ahead of Muddy Waters and Howlin' Wolf. But there are other ways to tell the story.

On 20 December 1938, Robert Johnson took the train from Memphis to New York City; later that week he performed "Terraplane Blues" and "Me and the Devil Blues" at Carnegie Hall. The next month he recorded with John Hammond for Columbia; the sessions, led by Louis Armstrong and featuring clarinet and trombone, were soon abandoned.

It wasn't Johnson's first time in Manhattan. As a traveling blues singer he'd been through Chicago and Detroit and played on the streets in Harlem. But in the audience at Carnegie Hall were the novelist and folklorist Zora Neale Hurston, the poet Langston Hughes, the future novelist Ralph Ellison, the heiress and ultrabohemian Nancy Cunard, the comic-strip artist George Herriman, and PaPa LaBas, the hoodoo theorist at the very center of the deep Harlem intelligentsia, who would turn up in 1972 as the hero of Ishmael Reed's novel *Mumbo Jumbo*. LaBas immediately recognized Johnson as a loa—a god that had to be fed, in this case with offerings of books, women, alcohol, and most of all, good company. After the performance LaBas brought Hurston and the rest backstage to meet Johnson; they left together and were soon inseparable.

In 1961, Hammond would tell Bob Dylan he was sure Johnson had read Whitman, and he was right—Johnson had based "Come on in My Kitchen" on both the Mississippi Sheiks' "Sitting on Top of the World" and "When Lilacs Last in the Dooryard Bloom'd." But in Harlem, in what amounted to a salon, Johnson read much more—Richard Wright's *Uncle Tom's Children* and *Native Son* (people got tired of Johnson getting drunk and announcing at every party, "*I* am Bigger Thomas!"), Hurston's *Hoodoo in Amer-*

ica and *Their Eyes Were Watching God* (no one got tired of him reciting, really half-singing, so quietly, "The wind came back with triple fury, and put out the light for the last time. They sat in company with the others in other shanties, their eyes straining against crude walls and their souls asking if He meant to measure their puny might against His. They seemed to be staring at the dark, but their eyes were watching God"), Hemingway's *The Sun Also Rises*, and his favorite, Fitzgerald's *The Great Gatsby* (unlike the poets in Greenwich Village bars, Johnson never raised his voice for the famous last lines of that one, but at any moment, apropos of nothing, he would simply proclaim, with endless delight, "Her voice was full of money!").

He performed for the salon, sometimes in clubs. He moved in with Cunard, just then getting over her breakup with the jazz bandleader Henry Crowder. Falling in with Bill Broonzy, he wrote part of what would become Broonzy's signature song, "Just a Dream"—the White House verse, which at first Broonzy didn't want to use. It was too much, he thought. It would break the everyday realism that underpinned everything else in the song, the verses about women, gambling, children—

I dreamed I was in the White House, sittin' in the president's chair

INSTRUMENTAL BREAK

I dreamed he's shakin' my hand, and he said, "Bob, I'm so
glad you're here"
But that was just a dream, Lord, now, what a dream I had on
my mind
Now, when I woke up, baby, not a chair there could I find

—when what the verse really did was rescue the song from
its own smallness. "'Dream,'" Johnson said, walking away,
leaving the song to Broonzy. "Dream *big.*"

In 1941, through Cunard, he met Harold Arlen and
Johnny Mercer, who already knew his "Hell Hound on
My Trail"; together they composed "Blues in the Night."
When the sheet music and the film with William Gil-
lespie's original recording appeared, there was no credit and
no money; Johnson complained. The publishing company
responded that Arlen and Mercer had never heard of
him—and while Bing Crosby sought him out to play guitar
for his recording of the song ("The only version," Johnson
would say, "worth worrying about"), it was a lesson he never
forgot.

When the war began, Johnson flew under the radar of the
draft. At the salon, he worked with Ellison on what would become *Invisible Man*—at first, Ellison had only the opening
lines, which he carried around like a tune he couldn't get
out of his head. He went to Buddy and Bob's on Lenox Ave-

INSTRUMENTAL BREAK

nue and bought the 78s of Johnson's records; "Dead Shrimp Blues," the song about impotence, scared him, and he played it only once, but he listened to the rest over and over again. At first, the song Ellison's underground man plays in his underground bunker with its 1,369 light bulbs running on bootleg electricity wasn't Armstrong's "What Did I Do to Be So Black and Blue," but Johnson's "If I Had Possession Over Judgment Day." Johnson suggested Geeshie Wiley's "Pick Poor Robin Clean," pulling the ten-inch disc out of a bag, telling Ellison she was the greatest blues singer who ever lived. The song stuck in Ellison's mind. It was a minstrel number; in 1930, with her partner Elvie Thomas, Wiley had tossed off its ugly lines with precisely the insouciant *fuck you* Ellison's hero, not to mention Ellison himself, would take years to grow into.

> Get off my money, and don't get funny
> 'Cause I'm a nigger, don't cut no figure
> Gamblin' for Sadie, she is my lady
> I'm a hustlin' coon, that's just what I am.

"But you need something people *know*," Ellison's editor told him ten years later, when the book was done. The editor knew his business; Ellison went for Armstrong, and that first scene struck a chord that rang down the years. But when Ellison reread the only novel he would finish in his lifetime, he still heard Wiley singing in those opening pages—and in 1962, ten years after *Invisible Man* appeared, in his essay "On Bird, Birdwatching, and Jazz," Ellison would use the song as a metaphor for the life and especially the afterlife of Charlie Parker, Bird picked clean by imitators and acolytes down to the bone.

After Cunard left Johnson for Bill Broonzy—Broonzy was much better looking—Johnson ended up in Los Angeles. He worked in Johnny Otis's band, learning the music business—learning firsthand from Otis, not as a mentor but by example, that you never let anyone know what you had, who you knew, or who you were: Otis, who ruled the world of race music in Los Angeles, whose title "the godfather of rhythm and blues" did not call up images of family picnics, was an olive-skinned Greek-American from Berkeley passing for black. He took a piece of every session, part of the publishing or even writer's credit on the songs that went through the studios he controlled. Johnson wrote for the band; he began producing records for people he heard in after-hours clubs. In 1948, after a year spent making a name and being held up for producer's fees and composer's royalties, he hired Easy Rawlins—the unlicensed private eye who specialized in cases of blacks passing for white and whites passing for black, and who in 1990 would appear in the first of Walter Mosley's detective novels based on his exploits—to unmask Otis. It took a week; Johnson always said it was the best $300 he ever spent. "But I've loved you ever since I heard 'Terraplane Blues' on the radio in Berkeley in 1936!" Otis said. "Love or money," Johnson said. "You can't have both."

After that, it was Johnson who held the gun on Otis. With the postwar shift from the likes of Otis's and Louis Jordan's big touring show bands to small harmony groups and solo singers, from race music to rock 'n' roll, from professionals to, so often, amateurs right off the street, Johnson took over as the producer to see in Los Angeles. He cut hits by Jesse Belvin, the Cuff Links ("Guided missiles, aim at my heart," he wrote for their hit "Guided Missiles." "Down to destroy me, tear me apart / Guided missiles, none of them true / Now I know, the enemy is you"), Etta James, Chet Baker, Richard Berry, and the early demo session on the jazz label Western Pacific for the Doors; the record he was most proud of was Ricky Nelson's "Poor Little Fool."

In 1961, John Hammond asked him to write the liner notes for the reissue of his 1930s recordings. He began with these ineffably Keatsian lines: "Robert Johnson is little, very little more than a name on aging index cards and a few dusty master records in the file of a phonograph company that no longer exists." He signed them "R. W. E."—for Ralph Waldo Ellison. *Invisible Man*—what could be more right than to disappear back into music he'd made so long before, into records he never talked about? "Look in your

phone book," he'd say on those rare occasions when someone asked if that was him. "There's a lot of Robert John-
sons." But for the reissue, he demanded copyrights, which
in the thirties nobody bothered with for race artists. Hammond, channeling the voice of his days as a pseudonymous
New Masses jazz critic—the John Hammond who, as it
happened, wrote under the name Henry Johnson, the John
Hammond who wrote that compared to Robert Johnson,
Lead Belly sounded "like an accomplished poseur"—said
he was sorry, but it was the system: *The same system that
kept your people in bondage after Reconstruction, and keeps
them in bondage today!* But the old record man was there
too. Hammond didn't mention that he would still collect
producer's royalties. By this time, Johnson had long since
learned that when you wanted something you couldn't
have, you needed the right lawyer. He went to see Clive
Davis, just hired as a twenty-eight-year-old assistant counsel
for Columbia. Davis agreed to make it happen—for a 25
percent silent-partner share.

Without the legend of a young man selling his soul to
the devil, Johnson's old music didn't become a cult, merely
a musician's talisman: Bob Dylan's "The stabbing sounds
from his guitar could almost break a window" was a common reaction. In 1969, as the blues historian Peter Guralnick once imagined, Johnson watched the Rolling Stones
play "Love in Vain" on the *Ed Sullivan Show*—though not,

as Guralnick also imagined, "on a TV he still owed payments on." He knew how much he was going to make off the song, for the rest of his life.

In 1931, scorned by the Clarksdale adepts, he'd spent a year with the older guitarist Ike Zimmerman near his birthplace in Hazelhurst. After long nights learning from Zimmerman as the two men sat on tombstones (in a cemetery owned by white people, Zimmerman's daughter Loretha K. Smith would say with glee more than eighty years later), Johnson made his return. Now it was Son House, Willie Brown, even Charley Patton who tried to watch his fingers, tried to understand how he did what he did; that was why Johnson turned his back, so no one could see. "They named my daddy the *devil*, because they felt like no human being could teach a person to play the guitar like that," Smith said. "But my dad, he wasn't the devil. He was a good man." After the war, Zimmerman moved to Compton, California, and opened his own Pentecostal church. In the 1960s he and Johnson joined hands once again. Johnson wasn't a believer, but he loved the fellowship. Among the friends he made were the Jacksons, the Youngs, and the Wrights—and, years later, long after Zimmerman's death in 1967, when Johnson was in his seventies and comfortably retired, O'Shea Jackson, Andre Young, and Eric Wright, remembering the family friend, the record man, sought him out, took him to swap meets and played him tapes, which is why, in

1988, when the boys were calling themselves Ice Cube and Dr. Dre and Easy-E, it was Johnson's name, one last producer's credit, that appeared on the back of N.W.A's *Straight Outta Compton*.

In the first years of the twenty-first century, people began to connect Mr. Johnson, the very old, very well-dressed man they'd see strolling the streets of Greenwich Village, sometimes stopping in at Evergreen Video on Carmine Street for *Homicide* sets (*That Andre Braugher*, he'd muse, thinking of women he met when he visited his half-sister in Baltimore, *sometimes he looks just like me*), the man who lived in a duplex on Washington Place and Sixth Avenue, right over the Radio Shack, with the Robert Johnson of those old index cards. Scholars sought him out. Books were published. He was interviewed on *Fresh Air*, and listened as hundreds of people recorded his songs. Thank God for Clive Davis.

He read some of what was written about him, but nothing really rang a bell until he picked up a copy of Bob Dylan's *Chronicles* from a used-books table up the block from his apartment. "I thought about him a lot, wondered who his audience could have been," Dylan wrote of the obsession that bloomed when he first heard *King of the Delta Blues Singers*. "It's hard to imagine sharecroppers or plantation field hands at hop joints, relating to songs like these." Johnson almost spit, thinking of the night in 1936 when a roomful of people broke into tears as he played "Come on in My Kitchen," but then he read the next line: "You have to wonder if Johnson was playing for an audience only he could see, one off in the future." Yes, he said out loud, thinking of the Dylan song he'd heard in a Victoria's Secret commercial. "Love Sick," that was it: "I'm walking"—that first line from the old Fats Domino hit, Johnson remembered— "through streets that are dead." That wasn't in Fats Domino. An audience far off in the future, he repeated to himself as he closed the book, and you were it.

On 21 February 2012, in his 101st year, he attended "Red, White and Blues" at the White House, and heard the president of the United States sing the last chorus of "Sweet Home Chicago." Six days later he saw the entire show— B. B. King, Buddy Guy, Susan Tedeschi, Warren Haynes, Jeff Beck, Booker T. Jones, and Mick Jagger (*he looks older than I do*, he thought)—broadcast on PBS. He called the White House to inquire about the royalty arrangements; finally he was put through to Jack Lew, President Obama's chief of staff. Lew was stunned. "Mr. Johnson," he said, "no one gets paid for playing for the president!" "Well, I don't know about that, son," Johnson said, "but there's one thing I do know. As the great Colonel Parker once said about his boy Elvis Presley, nobody asks Robert Johnson to play for nothing."

Money
(That's What
I Want)
1959·1963

Money
Changes
Everything
1978·1983·2008·2005

All rock 'n' roll songs about money, from the Drifters' "Money Honey" to Rubella Ballet's punk chant "Money Talks"—"In this/corrupt/society," Zillah Minx sings, breaking each word and each idea into its own line, "the rich/pay/to be free"— and on from there flow into Barrett Strong's "Money (That's What I Want)" or out of it. It was Berry Gordy's first hit on his own label; as Raynoma Gordy Singleton, his second wife and first partner in the enterprise that would become known as Motown Records, put it, with that song "we were really starting to be in the money." That was the meaning of the song as business. As something in the air, it wrote a bigger story: "Its immediate impact," Singleton said, "would be nothing compared to what it would do over the course of the decades to come."

Berry Gordy was born in Detroit; by 1959, just short of thirty, after dead-end careers as a boxer and a record store owner, he was making it as a songwriter. In 1957, along with his sister Gwen Gordy and the Chess staff writer Billy Davis, he'd written Jackie Wilson's signature "Reet Petite (The Finest Girl You Ever Want to Meet)," the first of dozens of Wilson numbers to make the national charts, and a year later co-wrote Wilson's "Lonely Teardrops," his first top ten hit. With Davis and Gwen he wrote Etta James's "All I Could Do Was Cry"—the three of them knowing, as James didn't, that her boyfriend, Harvey Fuqua of the Moonglows, was already deep into an affair with Gwen. The two were married the year after the record came out; when James said the song had played her for a fool, that was what she meant.

In Detroit, Berry's sister Anna already had her own label, Anna Records; Gordy and the then Raynoma Mayberry started Tamla. They named it for Debbie Reynolds's "Tammy": "We all really liked Debbie and that song," Raynoma Singleton wrote in 1990 in *Berry, Me, and Motown*, which some, aware of how quickly Berry Gordy's second wife became his second ex-wife and of how completely she was written out of the Motown story, translated as "Bury Me in Motown."

Late in 1959, Berry and Singleton watched as black, cutout cursive letters spelling "Hitsville, U.S.A." went up over the entry to a squat two-story house on West Grand Boulevard in Detroit. "Money" was the first record made there—or discovered there. As Singleton describes it, it is a rock 'n' roll origin story: another proof that rock 'n' roll can be born anywhere, at any time, regardless of how many times it might have been born before.

Gordy had Barrett Strong in the studio. Born in Mississippi in 1941, he was a songwriter more than a singer; with the Motown writer Norman Whitfield he would write a cornucopia of hits, including Edwin Starr's "War," the Temptations' "Just My Imagination (Running Away with Me)" and their epochal "Papa Was a Rollin' Stone," and "I Heard It Through the Grapevine," a song so rich that in 1968, a year after reaching number 2 in a version by Gladys Knight and the Pips that seemed to say everything the song had to say, it was an overwhelming seven-week number 1 for Marvin Gaye. Strong would make the national charts only once under his own name, but that one time has kept him on the radio all his life.

As Singleton tells the story, Gordy was at the piano, working on a riff from Ray Charles's "What'd I Say" as the songwriter Janie Bradford hung over his shoulder ("Her mouth was so murderous," Singleton writes, "that it could have had her arrested"). Strong sat down and he and Berry looked for a song together. Berry got up and let Strong go. "As soon as Barrett hit the groove," Singleton writes, "the sound vibrated up through the ceiling, right up into the room in which I was working and right into my bones. I bounded out of my seat to head downstairs."

> "What should we call it, what should we call it?" Berry was asking them.
> "Money!" Janie yelled out.
> "Yeah, you would say something like that," Berry laughed.
> "That's what I want," said caustic old Janie.

Soon they were improvising on a theme with Berry going, "Your love gives me such a thrill —"

And Janie answering, "But your love don't pay my bills." They kept bouncing these sassy phrases back and forth to each other.

I had now breezed into the studio, my heart doing pirouettes. Barrett had started singing too.

"Give me money," Berry blared. "That's what I want."

"That's . . . what I want," I echoed, carving out the soon-to-be immortal background vocal. Berry turned and smiled as he heard my voice. "That's the ticket."

They found a second verse. Singleton went back to her office to write out chord charts and call musicians. Over the next three days, with two guitarists, the bassist James Jamerson, the drummer Benny Benjamin, and three male backing singers plus Singleton, with one of them, Brian Holland, splitting the sound with a tambourine and Singleton conducting "like a traffic cop," with Gordy working on a three-track tape machine and Singleton losing count after forty takes, they made the record.

You can't hear it all at once. Strong leaps out into the music. Stopping each line like a car he's crashed into a wall —

The best things in life are free

— with a vehemence making each line simultaneously the beginning and the end of the story —

But you can give them to the birds and bees

—his voice is as harsh as the words he's singing, as violently emptied of compassion, empathy, trust, or warmth, as defiantly, proudly nihilistic. It is steely, honed, focused like a weapon on a single object, in Kara Walker's words "My Complement, My Enemy, My Oppressor, My Love": "Give me money." The rumble of the drums and bass could be coming from under the floor, and with such force it makes a swoosh as the instruments roll the melody over like a body.

The backing singers pull closer to each other with each line. Singleton's scratchy voice is dominating, piercing the sound of the men around her, the four pushing, as thrillingly autonomous as they are thrillingly anonymous, as if they are listeners shouting back at the radio rather than professionals inside a studio. Their satisfied, final, "That's what I want" sliding cynically off of the rushed, then bluntly dramatic "That's . . . what I want" now signifies what *these* singers want, the *I* redounding directly back on the woman's voice that for a moment has made you forget there's anyone else on the record.

You can see the people in the room, more people crowding in, until the riot inside bursts back out the door, people linking arms, running down the middle of the street, knocking over everyone in their path. The rhythm shifts unexpectedly, the sound rising and falling, and so starkly you can feel it all but disappearing into itself, then coming back, harder, because holding the world for ransom feels too good—until the end, when Strong breaks free of the role the song has given him, its demands really not who he is, or even what he really wants. He is someone else, more laconic, complacent, the battle already over: "All that lean green," he smiles, as if he's won the lottery, and the sting is gone. Go back and listen to him sing the first line and you can't believe it's the same person. It isn't: the song insisted he become someone else, and for just short of two minutes out of the two minutes thirty-five seconds of the record, he did.

In so many ways—for Motown, for the affirmation of noise, for speech that most of all wanted to please and speech that most of all wanted not to lie, for moving from "The Sound of Young America," as Gordy's future slogan would have it, to the sound of America plain and simple—the record drew a line: before "Money," and after.

In early 1964 a friend called people up and asked them if they wanted to hear the new Beatles album, *With the Beatles*. It had come out in the U.K. a couple of months before, but none of us in the U.S., our radios on all day for whatever Beatles song had broken into the Top 40 that week, had heard it, or for that matter heard of it. Our friend's father, an airplane pilot, had brought it back. We went to his house and looked at the four black-and-white faces on the cover—

John, George, and Paul on a top row, with Ringo, somehow smaller, alone below—with the left side of each face shaded so that it only half emerged out of the black behind it. The faces were impassive, looking straight back at whoever was looking at them. It was a design made to cast a shadow, and it did: in 2001, two days after George Harrison died of cancer at fifty-eight, twenty-one years after John Lennon was murdered at forty, Jim Borgman, the editorial cartoonist for the *Cincinnati Enquirer*, redrew the album cover, with John and George now returned to the blackness out of which they'd stepped so long before, only Paul and Ringo left. Their faces were still young, still looking out, now as faces recognizable everywhere in the world. They were unchanged as images but changed by the history they had passed through. They no longer seemed impassive at all, but questioning: *Was it worth it?*

Even in 1964, the feeling that came off the picture was unsettling: the jacket matched Beatles songs as they'd sounded a few weeks before in St. Michael's Alley, a coffeehouse that along with Kepler's Books constituted bohemia on the San Francisco Peninsula. It was days after the Beatles' first appearance on the *Ed Sullivan Show*. Up until then the place had played only folk music, maybe blues and hokum records from the twenties and thirties brought in by Jerry Garcia, who sometimes performed there with a jug band. This night "Don't Bother Me" felt like the spookiest song on earth.

Our friend played us the album, straight through to the last track, which, he announced, was the Beatles' version of "Money." And that, he said, would cost two dollars to hear. Per person: anyone not paying would have to leave. We paid. We listened. It would cost two dollars to hear it again, he said. We paid.

The Beatles loved Motown. They covered everything they could, even if it wasn't a hit, as "Money," issued in Great Britain in 1960, wasn't. So much the better: they could start a song from the ground up, take it to pieces, put it back as something new.

What they made in the studio on 18 June 1963 was the biggest sound imaginable. It wasn't pop. It wasn't entertainment. It was fun in the way that watching Michael Corleone shoot Sollozzo and Captain McCluskey is fun. It was shocking.

George Martin was the producer. He added Barrett Strong's piano part to the Beatles' recording after the fact, but the Beatles would have heard the piano as a ghost as they played. Certainly it was playing in John Lennon's head as he sang. The piano is a door to throw yourself against: a power source at the foundation of the song. Hearing the Beatles play the song onstage in Stockholm in 1963, two guitars, bass, and drums, you realize they don't need the piano, because as they hear themselves play, they feel Barrett Strong behind them. And behind Barrett Strong is another ghost.

In the brief tape made in Liverpool on 6 July 1957, the day the Quarry Men played on a truck and John Lennon met Paul McCartney for the first time, you can hear John copying Elvis's "Baby Let's Play House" and a Lonnie Donegan number, as other boys all over the U.K. were doing at the same time. As Devin McKinney has written, what's so uncanny about this recording is that, beneath the static and distortion, there is no question at all who is singing.

> After dark at that Woolton garden party of July 1957, Liverpool teenager and Lennon friend Bob Molyneux lifted the microphone of a Grundig recorder to the stage as John sang the new Donegan hit, "Puttin' on the Style." The tape that survives is a mere thirty-second shaving, and more than half its sound is surface noise, ambient racket, the cross-calls of Liverpool kids. You hear a hot, active summer night inside a provincial gymnasium. Pounded out for the dancing teenagers, the Quarry Men's beat is admirably certain, a consistent thud—the beat is really all there is to the music. Except for the ghost of Lennon's vocal: his sixteen-year-old voice, even half-heard, is simply not to be mistaken for any other. It flies like the cockiest, the looniest of birds over that low, dull thud; whines like a freighter steaming out of Liverpool Harbour.

The musical personality is strained, amateurish, shaky, not, in any formal sense, musical at all, but it is complete. You hear anger, resentment, discomfort, and determination

—and a will to inflict that anger, resentment, discomfort, and determination on everyone in the world. After six years of playing for yobs and screaming girls in Liverpool, for old Nazis and young Exis in Germany, this is what Lennon brings to bear on "Money," a song that wants all of those qualities as much as he wants the song. You can hear what the Beatles did with it as the only recording they ever made that truly captured the chaos of Hamburg, what happened in the fourth set of the night, maybe the fifth, when John put a toilet seat around his neck and all bets were off.

The performance is so fast, so big, relentless, and unforgiving it feels as if it's flying apart, two minutes and forty-nine seconds of the Big Bang in a box made of mastery and will. It is beyond belief that two guitars have built this wall of sound, but so much of what is happening is beyond belief; two months later the Rolling Stones would be recording their own version of "Money," but compared to the Beatles they were a skiffle band. You can only imagine how it made the Beatles feel to play this way, to find the pure pleasure of keeping every promise rock 'n' roll made to them when they first heard it, and then making it promise more than it ever had before.

The first words break the fanfare that opens the song; Barrett Strong is fierce, but John is appalled, hateful, and ravenous all at once, and so powerfully the music seems to fall away around him, letting him claim every molecule in the air for himself. The words begin to change: he puts so much pressure on *free* at the end of the first line it feels like death. He storms through the two-line verse, but Raynoma Singleton was right: it is the pause in her "That's . . . what I want" at the end of each chorus that seals the song. As she and the others sang it in Detroit, it was a whip cracking in the air; as Paul and George sing it, with the structure of the phrase now not made of wood but stone, that pause is frightening. It slaps back at the listener; you have no idea what's on the other side.

With the rhythmic force inside the song more impregnable with each measure, John can drive himself past anything the song has asked for, his *I can't use* so full of hysteria you can see the words bursting into flames as they leave his mouth, knowing that that force will always bring him back to the song. He knows that; you don't. The ground shakes; you are in a new world where values are shattering like plaster, honor, decency, fairness, kindness, and love replaced by sound and desire, and absolutely nothing else. As a face in the maelstrom John grows wilder and more crazed; as a singer the way he cuts phrases and bites off words becomes more strict and precise. Whether or not they recorded separately, I can only picture the moment as it would have taken place onstage: Paul and George put their heads to one mike to scream out a doubled *ooooooooo* so demonic it can make you flinch, not at the sound but at the wish for destruction it carries. Like John they are burning off their Beatle masks and raising the specter of a being so implacable it cannot be stopped and so consumed by urgency it can never be satisfied.

It powers on, until, near the end, Barrett Strong's coolly drawled lean green is replaced by a shout that is not musical, that is not part of the song, a cry that violates the rhythm that the Beatles have found in the song and that has given them the power to reduce Barrett Strong's record to dust. "I WANT TO BE FREE" John shouts off the beat, no longer hearing it, now merely an ordinary person utterly dwarfed by what the song has demanded, reduced almost to nothing in the face of the gauntlet the song has thrown against the world, and you realize that the person speaking will never be free. It is a record that in the years since it was made has lost none of its ugliness and none of its beauty.

A few months after I paid to hear the Beatles' "Money," I had it myself, on the Beatles' second Capitol album, so brilliantly titled *The Beatles' Second Album*. I was working in Washington, D.C., living in a basement in Chevy Chase with two roommates. They complained: why was I playing "Money" over and over? What was so great about it? I turned the sound up: *Look—here's what's happening. Wait for the instrumental break—now listen. Listen to what's going on. What you hear is a metaphorical representation of the out-of-control technological forces of modern society grinding the individual down to nothing. Do you hear that scream? That's the gears of the machine, destroying the soul!* I was laughing as I was talking, mocking my roommates' incomprehension and my own pretentiousness. But in the middle of it all I thought, why not? This makes sense. That's exactly what's happening. It was an argument about life—an argument that, onstage in Toronto in 1969, performing with others as the Plastic Ono Band, John Lennon made even more starkly, hammering the fanfare on his own guitar, when he already had more money than he would ever spend.

From its first line, as Berry Gordy and Janie Bradford wrote it, to its last line, as John Lennon rewrote it, this song is about nothing but freedom, and the acceptance, the insistence, that money is the only freedom there is or ever will be, the only form freedom can take or should. The Beatles give themselves over to this argument, and they hold nothing back. That's why listening to what they did that day in 1963 is like watching the best horror movie ever made, terrified of what's coming and unable to turn away.

"I came out of the fuckin' *sticks* to take over the *fucking world*," John Lennon once said. "Money" wasn't only what he meant, it was how the Beatles did it. "Philosophers have only interpreted the world," Marx said, "the point is to change it," and the purpose of "Money" was to change the world, to leave it different than it was before, as for Brian Epstein bigger, wider, less fixed and certain, and also scarier, more exciting, more emotionally and intellectually honest, more alive. But nearly twenty years later, when it was still impossible to write a song about money without thinking of what Barrett Strong or the Beatles had already done, the point for Tom Gray, teasing out the words and the melody of "Money Changes Everything," was to interpret the world. He did that, and with such ambiguous power that he set off a battle of the bands over a single song that is still going on today.

Tom Gray was born in 1951 in Washington, D.C., and grew up in Arlington and Atlanta; in 1978, a veteran of southern dance bands and trips to punk clubs in New York and Los Angeles with the Atlanta band the Fans, he had his metaphors lined up. He called his Atlanta punk band the Brains. He released "Money Changes Everything" as a 45 on his own Gray Matter label, with a gray label on the record itself. In the collaged band photo on the back of the sleeve, it was easy to pick out the leader: he was pasted in in front of the rest, a man with a high forehead, an accusing stare, and huge wire-rimmed glasses. As a name the Brains was more than funny, but Gray could have called the band the Philosophers and gotten it over with.

It was over soon enough. Though it never made the national charts, "Money Changes Everything" was inescapable across college and FM stations around the country. It got the band a major-label contract; they made two albums that went nowhere before they found themselves back in Atlanta and broke up.

"Money Changes Everything" as it first appeared remains a juggernaut. As with "Like a Rolling Stone" or "Light My Fire," there's a single snare shot, an announcement, and then instantly the event. An enormous sound appears, with a high, keening fanfare from Gray's organ, one note held down, others circling around it like crows. The cadence is crude, harsh, deliberate, as with Barrett Strong's "Money" aimed at a single target: the hell of other people. Gray's vocal was rough, without subtlety, a crying voice without the crying highs of a soul singer, self-pitying, stunned, the voice of someone disgraced by his own stupidity: he believed her when she said she loved him. He believed him when he said he was his friend. It's hard to believe the story even came through, it was so muffled as sound and ashamed as truth, but it did. It put you right in the singer's shoes, then tied them together and nailed the soles to the floor. After hearing the record once on the radio you could remember every word as if you'd heard the song all your life.

> She said I'm sorry, baby, I'm leaving you tonight
> I've found someone new, he's waiting in the car outside
> Oh honey how can you do it, we swore each other everlasting
>   love

She said yeah well I know but when we did there was one
    thing we weren't thinking of
And that's money
Money changes everything

The whole song turns on that smuggled *yeah*. Formally it's rhythmic filler; in the action of the music it's the reality principle of the song itself, a naturalistic epiphany for the songwriter passed on to the listener, a moment of coldness so absolute the singer knows there's not a word more he can say, a moment that tells the listener this story was over before the first word was all the way out of her mouth. And it's not even the cruelest moment. That comes at the end of the chorus, the woman looking back over her shoulder as she trips down the stairs, wanting one more look at the expression she's put on the man's face. "It's all in the past now," she says, and two hours later, he's still standing there, that look back turning him into a pillar of salt, not her.

The melody hidden in the cracks of the song, tiny guitar rhythms pulling against the theme repeated by the organ, made the words sail through the story like bullets, one following the other with the inevitability of time passing. Gray's voice started out strained, at the end he bellowed, but there was no melodrama. It didn't feel like a play. It was all artless, and covered with death. As the song careened toward the end—no comforting fade, but a clumsy, stuttering halt—you imagined what the man singing would do next: kill himself, or kill his mother, his father, and anyone else he could find. In some moods, listening, you can take the singer's rage for your own; in others, the music is lumbering, and the singer just another complainer, someone who never gets a break, someone who can tell you why it's never his fault, and you know too many people like that, and you might not want him around.

When Cyndi Lauper took the song up in 1983—during the sessions for *She's So Unusual*, her first album under her own name, an album that would produce five top five singles and make her a star—Ronald Reagan was in his third year of a presidency that had marshaled all the powers of his office to divide the country into winners and losers, and what Lauper heard in the song was not, you could think, what Tom Gray had ever imagined anyone might hear.

On the cover of her album, Lauper was posed on a New York street in front of signs reading THE WAX MUSEE, barefoot in a party dress, looking as if she were about to fall down; on the back of the sleeve she flew into the air, *Starry Night* reflected on the soles of her shoes as she rose into the sky. The pictures captured her life well enough. She was born in Queens in 1953. She left home at seventeen to escape a predatory stepfather, and knocked around New York and New England for the next twelve years, working dead-end jobs, eating badly and sometimes not at all, singing when she could, joining or forming bands, even putting out an album with one of them, leaving two rapes behind her, one by her own bandmates. In the studio, signed to Portrait, a small Columbia label, working with staff producer Rick Chertoff, she was looking for material: the company didn't trust her songwriting. She was almost thirty; she was no kid. She had never learned to keep her mouth shut, and with a first chance to say who she was and why anyone should care, it was the last thing she wanted to do. "Rick would play me 'Money Changes Everything' in the style of a Bob Dylan song," she wrote in 2012, "and I'd say, 'Can't we just start it off differently? Make believe you're playing 'London Calling.'" To her it was a Clash song, but no one else could hear what she heard. "I found myself trying to close my eyes and forget who I was," she wrote, "and try to find the spirit of the story—but there they were, watching me."

The song opens like a fire burning its way through a building, room by room as blowback shoots a woman and a man into the street. With the flames behind them—with Tom Gray's fanfare still holding the music in place, but with the there-is-nothing-new-under-the-sun bass line from Fleetwood Mac's "Go Your Own Way" at the heart of the sound—Lauper turns the song inside out.

I said I'm sorry baby, I'm leaving you tonight

Anybody else would have simply reversed the pronouns and made the victim female; Lauper sang not as a victim but as an avenger. As cold as Gray imagined the woman in his song, she is colder; the Queens so-what that makes her *yeah*

I said yeah well I know

snap in the air like fingers can stick in your mind like a curse you half remember, as if somewhere, sometime, someone said something in exactly that tone to you, and you're only now hearing it for what it was.

From a man's lament the song turns into a woman's manifesto. Glee drives the sound—*fuck you, loser*—and as the song goes on that *yeah* stays in the mind, changing shape, now not merely the coldest word in all of rock 'n' roll, but something worse, the sound of not caring. And then the word changes again, and it's worse than that, the sound of someone saying, I don't care, and I never did. The song echoes back through the century, maybe to its source: "Just tell him the truth—that you never loved him—and it's all wiped out forever," Gatsby says to Daisy, and what if she did? She could turn around and say the same about him to someone else, and she would, and he'd know it, and he'd lie awake thinking about it, living it out in advance, as long as she lay next to him. The song echoes back not to a source but to an American familiar always present whatever its form, here to Barbara Stanwyck in *Baby Face*, twenty-six as she walks in front of the cameras in 1933, her character maybe twenty as she appears on the screen. Pimped out by her father from the time she was fourteen, to escape Erie, Pennsylvania, where even with her father dead every mill worker knows her as a two-dollar whore, with the woman she's running with casting a cool eye on her she seduces a guard in a boxcar, then makes it to New York and with the camera panning up the side of an office building sleeps her way from the ground floor to the top in five minutes. There may be self-hatred in Lauper's voice, as there may be in Stanwyck's face, but there's more pride in both, and in the song as Lauper sings it even self-hatred, for the man a reason to crawl into bed and pull the sheets over his head, is one more engine: the sound is glamorous, not beaten.

At the end, bearing down on the chorus again and again, she begins to hold words. It seems like a device, something to dramatize passion, to fake it, and then the device explodes itself. With an intensity so great it is barely human, she holds the word *money* over the song for what feels like an impossible eleven seconds, the tone inside the word shifting, questioning itself, answering itself, deciding, and as the word does not fade but crashes down recommitting itself to the story the word is telling, the story of how, that night on the porch, the song became the singer's own declaration of independence, and she left everyone else, her one-time husband or lover and for that matter part of herself, the little girl who believed life could be any different, behind. A year later, with an adoring crowd at her feet, her eye makeup so smeared it looked as if she'd been beaten up, her hair flying, for "Money Changes Everything" she kicked a garbage can around the stage, and finally, still singing, she climbed into it. A hoist lifted her over the audience. Was she saying that Gray was right, that to take the role in the song that she did, trashing all values for the dollar, she had turned herself into garbage? It didn't matter if she was saying that or not. Flying over the crowd, she was still above it.

As the Beatles went beyond Barrett Strong, Cyndi Lauper went beyond the Brains. Listening to what she did with "Money Changes Everything," it's clear she owns the song, for good. She lives in its house. She might as well have her name on the deed.

Tom Gray didn't hear the story that way. As the years went on, Lauper's career faded. All too many people made her out as a brain to Madonna's bimbo, and, the right magazines said, "a real feminist"—after all, while Madonna was vamping around like a streetwalker, Lauper got "She Bop," a song about female masturbation, into the top ten. But by the time of "Like a Prayer," six years later, Madonna was breaking taboos as if she were following a script by Camille

Paglia and Cyndi Lauper was a face in the crowd. In 2003, Gray had formed a blues band called Delta Moon; by 2007, for the album *Clear Blue Flame*, the group was down to a core of the guitarist Mark Johnson and Gray playing guitar, dulcimer, and lap steel guitar, and Gray took up "Money Changes Everything" again. He looked like the Virginia banjoist Dock Boggs, less as he arrived in New York in 1927 to record Gothic blues and folk ballads than as he appeared forty years later, after the folklorist Mike Seeger found him living as a retired coal miner in the Appalachian mountains at the western tip of Virginia, and gave him a second public life at folk festivals from Newport to Berkeley. As Gray and Johnson recorded it, "Money Changes Everything" dried up quickly—but that same year, Gray appeared onstage in Atlanta, at a place called Club 29, to sing the song with the Atlanta punk band the Swimming Pool Q's, and he began to take it back.

It was an inflamed performance. If to festival audiences in the 1960s, an older, genial Dock Boggs didn't seem half as scary as he was, this night Gray was scary enough. He was thick in the face and around the waist, but in a way that signified resistance, not surrender. With the band to one side, he stood at the organ, playing with one hand, turning toward the crowd, his long gray shirt mottled with ugly sweat stains, his hair gray, looking as if he were fighting a war that should have killed him long before. Over a broken beat, he didn't so much sing the song as act it out, floridly, with stiff, clumsy gestures signaling an idea, a value, a violation, and it was, like Boggs's churning "Country Blues" or the demonic "Sugar Baby," a performance of guilt and death. Again, melodies crept out of the rhythm, gathering at the feet of the simple up-and-down fanfare Gray played on the organ, whispering, screeching, asking for more. The riff went right to the heart, and as the band bashes away there are moments when the music seems to pause and you hear a single musician, the guitarist, the drummer, emerge from the noise to say, yes, I hear this, I've lived this, I've died from this. Gray's singing is flat, there is no range, his voice is torn, he cannot lift his voice, and the melody and cadence he wrote into the song—now, its shudder—are so strong they carry him through it like wind. And a year later, in 2008, he was ready to do something he hadn't done before: to let the song speak through him, to listen to it as he sings, to let the song sing itself, with its writer its finder, its singer only a medium for any of the many things that, on any given night, the song might choose to say, with each note, each word, telling the next what to do, and why.

Delta Moon is playing the Melting Point in Athens, Georgia. For "Money Changes Everything," with Mark Johnson on electric guitar, Frahner Joseph playing bass, and Marlon Patton drums, Gray is holding an Appalachian dulcimer, standing up, bending his head toward his instrument. In 1927, the Brunswick label marketed Dock Boggs's records as Old-Timey; that's the sound that Gray, with a rolling, lyrical ensemble around him, has in his grasp now. The modal notes of a mountain ballad, "Little Maggie" or "East Virginia," emerge from the dulcimer, and the song starts up. The voice is as rough as it ever was, but you haven't seen this person before. He no longer looks like the middle-aged pharmacist on the back of last year's Delta Moon album. He's thin, and dressed the way the song now sounds, austere, spare, insistent, dignified, with a good haircut, a good-looking sports jacket, a good pair of trousers, a lawyer who's taken his tie off after work.

The notes coming out of the dulcimer are bright, high, and pretty, and all the more awful for that. The sound of the band is full, but the song as Gray shapes it gets smaller, quieter, and more hopeless than it ever seemed before, and Gray disappears into it, as angry as he ever was, or even angrier, because he knows what his anger will get him: nothing, other than another chance to sing the song. There was shell-shock on Gray's face when he began and acceptance when he finished; when he said thank you at the end it felt like he'd just confessed to a crime he didn't commit.

Two years later, it would be an act: Delta Moon as a three-piece, Johnson playing an acoustic guitar, Joseph a bass fiddle, Gray sitting down with a lap guitar on his knees, the three of them posing on a house porch, in the country, all but chewing on hayseed, playing "Money Changes Every-thing" old-timey style, not as sound but as a concept, and the song is dead. The song holds still for no one's museum. But Lauper had already claimed the territory.

In 2005, looking for a hook, an angle, a way back, late for the train of MTV's 1990s Unplugged shows, she redid her old songs for an album called *The Body Acoustic.* In the video she directed for "Money Changes Everything," six or seven musicians stand or sit on the steps of an old apartment house, with Lauper at the bottom, strumming a dulcimer, a harmonium in the hands of the man next to her, others with guitars, tambourine, dancing, clapping hands, your eye drawn most of all to the fiddler at the top, one Allison Cor-nell. She kicks off the music, which is immediately seized by a bass drum sound so big the hidden instrument might as well be the building itself, and then the steps are filled, the crowd more than doubled, until it looks and feels like the whole town is there to sing this old-timey song. Lauper rags the tune, letting her voice fall behind the beat—it's a singalong, good-time music, how can a feeling so right leave anyone without a smile? And then Cornell, her head shaved to a burr, a knowing look on her face, swoops into a solo, and the song is startled into a different life.

Now the only language it speaks is the language of mourning, pain, desperation, and defeat. It's all in the tone, and the tone is there from the first note: you're no longer in the Virginia mountains, you're in a cabaret in Central Europe, Café America, sometime in the thirties, maybe Munich, maybe Budapest, maybe Prague, and with you in the crowd are Weill and Brecht, Fassbinder and Hanna Schygulla, Eric Ambler's Soviet spies Tamara and Andreas Zaleshoff and Philip Kerr's Berlin cop Bernie Gunther, all contemplating the compromises they've already made, figuring their chances of coming out on the other side of the next war, Cornell's sound as serious as night, and when the song comes back to Lauper it has changed. There's still comfort, even joy, in the way the melody sways in the trees, in the heart everyone puts into the music, but the old folk wisdom the tune is carrying is all shadows and hideouts. This is life, and there's nothing you can do about it. Life, as Fitzgerald said in a line he didn't give to Gatsby, is essentially a cheat, but we're together, and no matter what the words we're singing say, the rhythm comes first. The story we're telling is about imprisonment, but the music we're making is about freedom, the tiny moments of freedom you steal from a life you don't own, that doesn't belong to you, that you have to live.

At the end of the song Lauper begins to shout. With a late, 1960s doo-wop scratch in her throat, more Reparata and the Delrons than the Shirelles, she can't hold *money* the way she once could, but she can push it, stretch it, hammer it, try to break it, blow it up like a bomb, turn it into a nursery rhyme, play the word as if she were a horn, embrace the word, the idea, the life as completely as Barrett Strong did at the end of his song, *money money money money money money money*, twenty times that feel like more than anyone could count.

This "Money Changes Everything" tells Neil Young's story: rock 'n' roll comes first, blues and country only later. How strange that, for both Tom Gray and Cyndi Lauper, a song they had fought over for twenty-five years and may be fighting over for years to come should finally find its way back into a body, a host, so unlike the punk body of noise, force, and defiance that, for both of them, the song started with: the body of an old folk song, a song people were singing long before either of them were born, a song with no original and thus no copy. The point, they found, was to play this song as if it had always existed, their task simply to keep it alive, to pass it on. And, in its way, in the conversation rock 'n' roll has with itself and with the world at large, the same thing has happened with "Money."

In the movie *Killing Them Softly*, released in 2012, it's 4 November 2008, and with a 1930s version of "It's Only a Paper Moon" floating over him like a cloud, Brad Pitt's hitman walks into a bar to meet mob fixer Richard Jenkins to collect for the three people he's killed. Jenkins is trying to short Pitt on the price; on the TV monitor above them, Barack Obama is giving his victory speech. "Ah, yes, we're all the same," Pitt says. "We're all equal." "We have never been just a collection of individuals or a collection of blue states and red states," Obama says. "We are, and always will be, the United States of America." Pitt puts a cigarette in his mouth. "Next he'll be telling us we're a community, one people," Pitt says. "In this country," Obama says, "we rise or fall as one nation, as one people." "We're one people?" Pitt says. "It's a myth created by Thomas Jefferson." "Now you're going to have a go at Thomas Jefferson," Jenkins says. "My friend," Pitt says quietly, like a professor talking to a student. "Jefferson's an American saint, because he wrote the words all men are created equal—words he clearly didn't believe, because he allowed his own children to live in slavery. He was a rich wine snob who was sick of paying taxes to the Brits. So yeah, he wrote some lovely words and aroused the rabble and they went out and died for those words, while he sat back, and drank his wine, and fucked his slave girl." He points up at the TV, his voice quieting even more. "This guy wants to tell me we're living in a community? Don't make me *laugh*. I'm living in *America*, and in America you're on your own. America's not a country. It's just a business. Now *fuckin'* pay me." Then the screen goes black and on the soundtrack Barrett Strong takes the story from there.

This
Magic
Moment

2007·1959

On 22 July 2007, in Prospect Park in Brooklyn, Lou Reed took the stage to close a tribute to Doc Pomus, a songwriter who had died sixteen years before, in 1991, at sixty-five. Born Jerome Felder in Brooklyn in 1925, he was six when he contracted polio; by the late 1940s he was performing in New York clubs, a Jewish blues singer on crutches. The records he made were distinctive, but they didn't sell. He had been composing songs for himself; writing alone or with partners, he began to offer his tunes to others, and wrote history, especially with Atlantic Records. He wrote "Lonely Avenue" for Ray Charles, "Young Blood" for the Coasters, "Viva Las Vegas," "Little Sister," and "Suspicion" for Elvis Presley, "There Must Be a Better World Somewhere" for B. B. King, and most memorably, for the Drifters, "Save the Last Dance for Me," "I Count the Tears," and "This Magic Moment." Sitting heavily in his wheelchair with a fedora and a cigar, he was a ladies' man, a legendary raconteur, a constant mentor, a beloved friend. "If the music business *had* a heart," Jerry Wexler once said, "it would be Doc Pomus."

Lou Reed had himself recorded "This Magic Moment" in

1995 for *Till the Night Is Gone,* a Doc Pomus tribute album. Contributions included Bob Dylan on "Boogie Woogie Country Girl," originally written for Big Joe Turner; after I reviewed a 1970 version by the now-forgotten Southwind in *Rolling Stone,* Pomus, who I'd never heard of, was on the phone for over an hour, at first haranguing me for failing to mention who'd written the song, then talking about how songwriters never got credit for anything ("People think the *artists* write the songs!" he said with utter incredulity), then talking about everything under the sun. The highlight of the album was a crawling version of "Viva Las Vegas" by Shawn Colvin, singing as a hooker just after being pushed down the stairs from the escort service to the street. Reed took "This Magic Moment"—with the tenor Ben E. King in the lead, a number 16 hit for the Drifters in 1960, a Velveeta number 9 in a 1968 cover by Jay and the Americans, taken up lifelessly by Marvin Gaye in 1969 and Rick James twenty years after that, but never altogether off the air or out of mind—as if the challenge was to retrieve the Drifters' sense of wonder from the dank pit of hipster cynicism where Reed had buried it long before. But his heart wasn't in it—that was the drama he played out as he sang. It wasn't that the singer couldn't believe the love-will-never-die promises of the song; he didn't want to, and to disguise that pain, Reed's performance was a study of cool. The recording only came to life a year later, when David Lynch used it to orchestrate that moment in *Lost Highway* when the mobster's lover played by Patricia Arquette gets out of a black Cadillac convertible in an auto garage and, in super-slow-motion, passes under the gaze of Balthazar Getty's mechanic, and stops him cold. *Look out look out look out!* the song says as Reed shreds it on his electric guitar. *You'll never get her face out of your head! You'll never get out of this song alive!*

"These are a few words, last words for tonight, from the great man, Doc Pomus," Reed said in Brooklyn. He held up a page and read. "'The important thing is to be the poet. Not the famous poet. There's so many uncontrollable intangibles that make up recognition and success. It's the life we choose that sets us up, in the hierarchy of humans, that proves our courage and understanding, and sensitivity. I'd rather be the worst poet than the best agent.'" "It gives me great pleasure," Reed said, "to bring in Ben E. King. 'This Magic Moment.'" You can hear what he said more plainly, and more personally: "Ben E. King. This magic moment."

At sixty-six, dressed in a dark suit and an open-necked white shirt—a far cry from oldies performers at oldies revues, with their Omar-the-Tent-Maker stage suits in garish colors and tails and ruffled shirts—King looked ten years younger, handsome and confident. He could have been a former ballplayer now doing color commentary for ESPN. But you couldn't tell: he also looked like an alcoholic dragged out of a shelter and cleaned up for the night.

With that jolt of realism in his appearance, he led the crowd in slow clapping. He sang very carefully, fitting his voice to the original cadence of the song—but, really, too carefully, not sure, in the moment, that he could climb the steps of the rhythm. Then the tension eased, and he began to stretch the song out, not to let it end, barely to let it begin, the whole performance an introduction to a book it was forbidden to open.

He could be preaching. The music is faint; then there's a high, grating gypsy violin, an intrusion, then pizzicato, which settles the tone. But there is jeopardy in each measure of the song—something of the feeling that sneaked out when Reed had played it twelve years before—and with each sung line you can feel the song fall through the cracks, the cracks of real life. Even when the song first appeared on the radio, the most swooning listener knew that "This magic moment . . . will last forever/Forever till the end of time" wasn't true, but you let it go—after all, it was just a song. But now you can't let it go. You can't not hear, behind the words Pomus wrote with his partner Mort Shuman, their own cynicism, and as he sings King hears that too—that was the drama that, this night, he played out.

Sadness and knowledge—Bob Seger's wish-I-didn't-know-now-what-I-didn't know-then—flood the quiet performance, but it doesn't feel like a performance. It feels like a confession, a wish to be forgiven for propagating the myth that the song could be true.

He takes his time. Bowing his head, holding the microphone with his right hand and clenching the fist of his left, then touching his chest in time, still not lifting his head, King speaks to the song. "Oh, magic moment," he says, as if it is a person, with its own will, its own failures, its own cruelty. "Say magic," he pleads, then letting the words explain themselves: "Say, 'magic moment,'" but the words refuse to answer back. Now the performance is a séance. Watching the words dance around him, he stays with the theme for a whole minute, then lets the words dance him off the stage.

The surge of the original arrangement and what it once brought out of him are completely gone, and that's the point, in a way that's the satisfaction—to have outlived the song, to have solved its mystery and escaped its spell—but still, he's going to let this boat drift all the way down the river. His swollen face looks bruised from the inside. Now, as he disappears into shadows of the stage, he could be Rabbit Brown, serenading sweethearts on Lake Pontchartrain in 1927 with the minstrel bounce of "Never Let the Same Bee Sting You Twice" or the quiet, rippling *bump-baa*'s of his "James Alley Blues." He could be Joe Louis in 1955, once the greatest prizefighter of his generation, a national hero for his defeat of the so-called Nazi puppet Max Schmeling in 1938 ("I wouldn't even pay my house rent/Wouldn't buy me nothing to eat," Memphis Minnie sang: "Joe Louis says, 'Take a chance with me/I'll put you on your feet'"), now a greeter at a Las Vegas hotel—at the Moulin Rouge, the first hotel on the Strip to admit black people. "We're not trying to prove anything here," Louis said; it had been four long years since taxes forced him back into the ring and the whole world saw Rocky Marciano knock him out. "First of all we are in business to make money. If it helps the racial situation here in Vegas, so much the better."

The year before, in 1954, with *Brown v. Board of Education*, the Supreme Court ruled segregation in public schools unconstitutional. By an implication that has never been settled, the unanimous court said that all racial segregation violated some essential premise of American life, that it was a crime against the very idea of an American identity. Six months after Joe Louis helped open the Moulin Rouge in Las Vegas, the NAACP activist Rosa Parks refused to give up her seat on a bus to a white man and was arrested, and the Montgomery Bus Boycott, with a then-unknown preacher named Martin Luther King, Jr., as its commanding voice, upended the city and sounded a call that echoed across the country. With that and *Brown*, the words *civil rights* began to enter the national conversation. By 1959 it was the ruling question of national life: would America live up to its promises, or deny that they had ever been made?

The resignation and sorrow over how incomplete that answer would turn out to be is in "This Magic Moment" as

Ben E. King sang it in Brooklyn in 2007, with a black community once vitalized by a mission that was both spiritual and political long since smashed by the unapologetically racist backlash of the Nixon and Reagan administrations, by the drugs, gangs, and casual murder those years left as the fastest route to self-affirmation, and maybe the surest. The sound of a different notion of self-affirmation—of people feeling themselves on the verge of remaking both their country and themselves—is in "This Magic Moment" as the Drifters recorded it on 23 December 1959.

Nine months earlier they had made "There Goes My Baby." Though as a name on a record label the Drifters went back to the early 1950s, to the impishly sexy lead singing of Clyde McPhatter and such glorious Atlantic hits as "Money Honey," "Let the Boogie Woogie Roll," "Honey Love," and a zoot-suiter's transformation of "White Christmas" that made Irving Berlin smile, after McPhatter left the group it withered into hack work. The Drifters' manager, George Treadwell, owned the franchise; he fired those who were left and made a deal with one Lover Patterson, the manager of a group called the Five Crowns. With their lead singer Benjamin Nelson—the sharper monicker Ben E. King would come later—the Five Crowns became the new Drifters. Nelson—King—was born in Henderson, North Carolina, in 1938; from the age of nine he grew up in Harlem. Now, with the shell of a famous group to fill, he cradled his guitar and sketched out a song. With final credit going as well to Patterson, Treadwell, and Jerry Leiber and Mike Stoller, who produced it, "There Goes My Baby" made the world forget anyone else had ever called himself a Drifter.

It bore no resemblance to any record that had had the name Drifters on it; it bore no resemblance to any rock 'n' roll record anyone had ever made. Inside the song was something more than a song, something closer to an epic; to bring it out, Leiber and Stoller hired a conductor and ten string players. There had been violins and cellos on rock 'n' roll hits before; the Platters were using them on anything that moved. It was the standard way to shift a teenage idol into the nightclub market. Buddy Holly recorded a slew of hearts-and-flowers arrangements in 1958. But this sound wasn't pretty; it wasn't sweetening. It wasn't nicely coiffed hair, capped teeth, and a polite knock on the door. It was bad weather: huge, sweeping, dark, harsh, and threatening. In America as it was chronicled in the Top 40, the record was a foreign country: an intrusion of the blues, a sign of the adult world that from its first bars enacted what it signified. As so many people said, it sounded like the radio dial was stuck between two different stations; it sounded like an accident, a mistake, a collision of songs that had been floating in time since the first radio signal went into the ether.

It was an epochal hit. Like Bob Dylan's "Like a Rolling Stone" six years later, officially it reached no higher than number 2, but in fact it was, in its moment, the only song anyone really heard, number 1 in the form of an idea that outweighed any facts. The music was new. It was bigger than life, it could feel, but then, as the record grew in strength every time it was played, bigger than that: as big as life.

Like Elvis Presley's "Heartbreak Hotel" in 1956, the Kingston Trio's "Tom Dooley" in 1958, or Nirvana's "Smells Like Teen Spirit" in 1991, it made everything else on the radio seem beside the point. Elsbeary Hobbs curled his bass voice around the opening doo-wop phonemes—

Bomp baa

—which as Dock Green, Charlie Thomas, and Johnny Lee Williams came in, their last two syllables falling away from the four that preceded them like bodies thrown overboard—

Do-doot
Do do
Do do

—rose up to take the shape of something more dramatic than such sounds had ever described before, raising the curtain for King's heroic lead. "There goes my baby, moving on, down the line"—an image opened up, of men and women shuffling out of the light and into obscurity, the singer seeing his whole life, past, present, and future, fading before his eyes, following the shadow of the woman walking away from him until, finally, he saw himself in that same line, and heard someone else singing the song about him, heard someone forgetting his face, forgetting his name.

It set the commercial template: now Drifters records had strings. The weak "Dance with Me"—weak as an idea, tame as a sound—followed, stopping at number 15. A year would go by until Pomus and Shuman's "Save the Last Dance for Me" reached number 1. But in between they brought in "This Magic Moment." Though it would chart one place lower than "Dance with Me," it would speak the new language the songs were making more clearly and more fully than any other record.

King doesn't stride into the song. From his first word he is present at its center. It could be a common dream in which he has found himself exposed and must account for himself. The voice he's speaking in could have come from Doc Pomus and Mort Shuman, King's own memories, the hopes of an entire people, God, or the look that Tom Dowd, the engineer on the session, was throwing his way. Regardless of who writes it, no successful song is a memoir, a news story, and no such song does exactly what its author—and that can be the writer, the singer, the accompanist, the producer—wants it to do. One must draw on whatever new social energies and new ideas are in the air—energies and ideas that are sparking the artist, with or without his or her knowledge, with or without his or her consent, to make greater demands on life than he or she has ever made before.

That is true for the songwriter; it's true for the singer. The song, as Louise Brooks liked to quote "an old dictionary" on the novel, "is a subjective epic composition in which the author begs leave to treat the world according to his point of view," but the song, as it takes shape, makes certain things rhythmically true and others false, makes certain phrases believable and others phony—and someone speaking to the world by himself or herself is never solely that. Other voices, those of one's family and musical ancestors, other singers competing on the charts, movie characters, poets, historical figures, present-day political actors, are part of the cast any good song calls up, and calls upon.

"I wrote 'Gimme Shelter' on a stormy day," Keith Richards wrote in 2010. "I was sitting there," he said, speaking of the Swinging London scenemaker Robert Fraser, "just looking out of Robert's window and looking at all these people with their umbrellas being blown out of their grasp and running like hell. It was a shitty day. I had nothing better to do . . . I wasn't thinking about, oh my God, there's my old lady shooting a movie in a bath with Mick Jagger. My thought was storms on other people's minds, not mine." But it was 1968, when, while recording "Sympathy for the Devil," the Rolling Stones had to change "Who killed Kennedy" to

"Who killed the Kennedys." It was a year when Richards's picture of umbrellas being blown out of people's hands could serve as a metaphor for the demonstrations against the war in Vietnam, on a deeper level against life as it was then lived and administered, spread from the U.S. to the U.K. In France and Czechoslovakia, governments, the very legitimacy of state power, shook, and many were sure they were only days from toppling. All of that is in "Gimme Shelter"—as it was made, and as it was heard. What has kept it on the radio for more than forty-five years is its music, and the unsatisfied history it carries with it. Who's to say Ben E. King didn't name himself after Martin Luther King? Not Ben E. King (*I had an uncle everyone called "King"—it sounded cool*). D. H. Lawrence's "Never trust the teller. Trust the tale" is always right.

Are you sure? says the look from Tom Dowd to Ben E. King. He is barely twenty-one, but he has to be sure. In the studio there may be as many takes as they need to get it right, but in the real life of the song this is the only chance to say it all, to say what's never been said, for the singer to position himself against the cheat of life and win. He sounds as if he's giving a speech. There's a certain stiffness, a stentorian hesitation before each phrase, something built into the stop-time Brazilian baion rhythm as it's lined out by almost subliminal acoustic guitars and bass fiddle, that gives the whole performance a humanness, a sense of contingency, a smell of fear underlying the bravery that shoots out of every word King shapes in his mouth: "different," "new," "until," "and then it happened." The performance is a dare, made as much of nerves as heart. The singer could be running for office, fully conscious of how young he is, aware that people won't take him seriously, that he will have to make them believe what their faces tell him they will never believe, but absolutely convinced of his right, duty, and ability to serve.

He is not singing his life—not like someone in that very moment offering a short story in the Writers' Workshop at the University of Iowa. He is not necessarily singing what he knows. For that matter, there is no reason to think Doc Pomus and Mort Shuman were writing their lives or their experiences or even their desires and fears. They are professional songwriters trying to get another record made, to write another hit in the mold of previous Drifters hits. They are plugging into an established format of romantic ballads. But at the same time, both they and the Drifters, and especially Ben E. King, writers and singers with an inherited repertoire of gestures and vocal signifiers, are entering a constructed, fictional situation where they have to feel their way as if in the dark.

Here, in this new country, each word, each note, will suggest what might come next, what should, what could. The risks of failure in each choice increase from might to should to could—what could you say, what could you feel, what sense of life could you pass on to others, what could you do that hasn't been done before? To essay this, the writers and actors in this drama do have to draw on their experiences, their desires, their fears—consciously, subconsciously, cynically, with a sense of awe at what is coming out of their mouths as the songwriters sit at the piano in their Brill Building cubicle and Ben E. King stands isolated in the Atlantic studio, each one discovering both the song and himself, his own limits and his will, and his ability, to transcend them. "Along with a strong ethic in the power of individual performance," the critic and guitarist Lenny Kaye wrote in 2001, "came Atlantic's belief in the power of the musician's instinct, always pushing the tape level to catch the wobble behind the note, the string moving just that extra millimeter higher, the rhythm in sharp focus even as you can hear a musical mind setting up the next phrase of the chords. The needs of the song were always held paramount, and the catchy three or four note melodies and backbeat then parted to make way for the singer: always the singer."

As the song opens, it's cotton candy—and then for all the gravity King brings to the performance as soon as he opens his mouth, it could be Lincoln trying to explain justice to a crowd, whether it's a few layabouts in New Salem, Illinois, in 1832, or the African-American Union soldiers in the front rows for his second inaugural in Washington, D.C., thirty-three years later. There's a rush of high, keening violins, the strings running away from each other until they're cut off just like that. "This magic moment," King announces, each word bigger, more fully shaped and with more body, than the one before it. He doesn't need more words; he could chant those words all the way through the song. The strings reemerge, but the guitars and bass carry more of the music, tracing a melody and a syncopated rhythm that go straight back to Dean Martin's "Memories Are Made of This," number 1 for six weeks over the end of 1955 and the beginning of 1956.

It's a piece of music so delicate and strong that in the 1990s Nan Goldin could use it to validate the closing montage of *The Ballad of Sexual Dependency*, her slide-show portrait, taking shape from the late 1970s into the 1990s, of a family of friends "only satisfied by love, heroin, or chocolate": an old man in a coffin, a blonde woman you've seen before passing in front of it, then the woman in her own coffin, no direct references to AIDS or an overdose, but any of that subsumed in the visual rhythm of connection, isolation, and memory. So there is a heart-shaped frame holding the portrait of a couple, a framed picture of hearts and before it a vase of flowers and a medicine bottle, an empty bed with tangled sheets, a bedroom wall splattered with blood, and then tombstones, a whole forest of mausoleums, and, as the very last image, a crude painting on the door of a shed of two skeletons making love standing up. Over it all hovers the lightness and the strength of Dean Martin's song, the chorus murmuring, Martin finding soul in the slide of the verses, the music endowing everyone you've seen with dignity.

That lightness, that strength, hovering over anyone's everyday life like a cloud, is what Ben E. King is reaching for. That's what he finds and what, as his song reaches its end, he never surrenders. The other Drifters are barely there at all, merely another element in the sound. Even when, after the instrumental break, the rhythm the strings are making cuts back against itself, against the singer, forcing him to make his words swim upstream against the melody, King betrays no doubt. The delicacy in the way he handles Pomus and Shuman's shopworn "sweeter than wine" is confirmed with the awe he gives their startling "Everything I want I have." The force King puts into the line is so great that there is no chance that what he wants, what he has, will itself ever grow shopworn—this is a moment, not a life, a moment rescued from life, the moment you return to when life itself turns the truth of the feeling with which King endows the words into the lie the words contain. But you don't have to hear any of that.

In *AKA Doc Pomus*, a documentary film from 2012, you see a hand go to a car radio dial. The critic Dave Marsh is talking: "You've got a radio on, right? And what's coming across, most of the time, frankly, is static and nothing. And then, this *thing*—and that's the Drifters." On the soundtrack, "This Magic Moment" begins to play. There's a close-up of the Atlantic label with the song title and the writers' names as Marsh goes on: "And that's Doc Pomus, that's Mort Shuman, and it's Jerry Wexler and Ahmet Ertegun, and Tom Dowd, and all the people who recorded it, and then ultimately, that's you and me."

What it is, coming out of and entering into all of those people in a swirl of transubstantiation, is soul music, here taking a shape so stark that it makes the style, in the deepest sense of the word, turn around the record as if that seven-inch disc were the sun, with the first, struggling attempts in the 1950s to discover the music—Ray Charles's "What Would I Do Without You," the Chantels' "If You Try," the Five Keys' "Dream On"—and the deep-soul records of the mid-'60s that can seem to take the style, now a form, as far as it could go—Irma Thomas's "Wish Someone Would Care," Otis Redding's "Try a Little Tenderness," and Percy Sledge's "When a Man Loves a Woman," Aretha Franklin's "I Never Loved a Man the Way I Love You," Lonnie Mack's "Why," most of all Sam Cooke's "A Change Is Gonna Come"—the planets that circle it. And because soul music is the limitless affirmation of the individual despite his or her past sins and all obstacles in his or her way, an affirmation that remains even in the moment before suicide, as it can seem to be in "Wish Someone Would Care" and "Why," each of these records can, in the moment in which you hear them, be the sun, and all the rest, "This Magic Moment" spinning with them, again mere planets, maybe even, someday, should they ever fade, and their lies speak more loudly than whatever truths they tell, written out of the book and taken down from the sky, like Pluto—except that once a song has gone into the ether, it never disappears.

Guitar Drag

2006·2000

I t's 2013, maybe 2014. You walk into one of the vinyl shops that are beginning to dot cheaper commercial neighborhoods—the Lower East Side in New York, Skid Row in Seattle, West Hollywood, maybe Stranded on Telegraph Avenue in Oakland. In a used bin you find a twelve-inch disc with a blurry photo on the cover. You can see rope and some kind of machinery. You turn the sleeve over and on the back there's a distorted but decodable picture: what seems to be an electric guitar with two leads attached, one taut, one loose, on a brown surface that might be a road. There are no words or even lettering on either side; the spine reads "Christian Marclay   Guitar Drag   Neon Records." You pay $7.95—"It's pristine," says the guy at the counter—take it home, slit the shrink wrap, take out the record, put it on your turntable, info label side up: "Soundtrack from the video Guitar Drag, 2000. Recorded San Antonio, Texas, on November 18th, 1999. Released by Neon Records, Sweden 2006." You cue it up and the tone arm slides right to the label. You adjust the weight and try again, with the same result: there are no grooves on the record. You turn it over, where the label again shows the blurry photo—now you can see the six tuning pegs of a guitar, a rope around the top of the neck, and a dirt road. 33 RPM, it says. Now it plays.

At first there's silence, then intermittent rumbling noises, scraping noises, the noise of something hollow. After a minute, you catch the high pings of a guitar being tuned, then feedback turning into a whine, bass strings being fingered, a quiet strum on the strings that echoes into more feedback, making a sound far too big for whatever it is you're picturing as the action behind what you hear.

At two and a half minutes there's the unmistakable sound of a car starting—the only unmistakable sound, it will turn out, that you'll hear. Immediately a harsh noise kicks up, relentless, monochromatic; then a second noise, higher, then under the surface of the first two tones a bass counterpoint, so much bigger than the other sounds it almost drowns them out, then a treble sound raised over the others and held.

Another minute and a half has gone. The higher tone has shifted under the lower. The harsh noise has disappeared. Then the guitar begins to screech and reach; you can feel it trying to make a chord. There's a bass rumble, then a scramble, the pace picking up: the simultaneous levels of sound are constantly changing position, fighting for primacy, bass versus treble, treble versus bass, scattered noise versus steady tone. You try to make a narrative out of it all, to see the music, because it is beginning to come across as some kind of music, going somewhere. Guitar Drag? For a moment you forget the label you read: maybe that's the name of the band, a drone band like Th Faith Healers, with their mesmerizing thirty-two minute "Everything, All at Once, Forever," which pretty much covers the territory. You hear the car engine again, revving up, increasing speed, until it vanishes under a furious sonic back-and-forth, yes no yes no yes no, that breaks any picture you were trying to make.

At seven minutes, the sound begins to fade, or seems to — the piece, or the documentary recording, or the computer manipulation, whatever it is you're listening to, seems to assume a kind of shape. If you can't find a story in the noise, or make one up, you can get used to the noise, stop hearing it, erase the story you can't decode. The sound rises slightly, more modulated, less frantic, dissonant but with direction. Then the noise doubles into a high screech, then it narrows, so that there's less to hear, and then you're looking straight into a chainsaw, everything cut and torn apart, then quiet, an object being pulled through water or gravel, and then a surge of speed and volume, then the volume up and the speed down, a moment of suspense, a breath drawn, and at eleven minutes you don't like where this is going.

Before that sensation can turn into a thought, the terrain the sound is making is invaded by the loud, focused sound of something boring into something else. Everything begins to break up. Even in the chaos you get used to it. The sound isn't quieter but it seems to be. The boring noise recedes, replaced by a high scratch, the sound band narrowing even further as the car again picks up speed, even sounds, feels as if it's swerving from one side of the sound, or the road, to the other. With the screech constant, for the first time you begin to hear as if you're listening from inside of the noise as it happens, as it is made, as it occurs—no epistemology rules any more than any sound does, but what you're hearing is alive, trying to speak, trying to form a language.

You can distinguish three levels of sound. As at the start there is rumbling, feedback, but without a sense of movement, a slowing down, the sound narrowing from a dark mass to a single line drawn in pencil down a page. The sound holds, and, at just over fourteen minutes, it disappears.

Colson Whitehead's novel *John Henry Days* centers on vastly different appearances of the ballad about the race between the great steel driver and the steam drill built to replace him, the story of how John Henry beat the machine at the cost of his own life: of how, as countless singers black and white have sung, from some time in the 1870s or the 1880s to this day, "he laid down his hammer and he died." Parading through Whitehead's pages are an unnamed singer searching the old song for new words, the Tin Pan Alley song plugger who at the start of the twentieth century becomes the first man to copyright it, a Mississippi blues singer recording it in Chicago in the 1930s, a crackhead singing it on the street in the 1990s. Alternating with their stories are the cynical adventures of a hack journalist named J., on a junket to Talcott, West Virginia, one of various places where the great race was supposed to have taken place in the years after the Civil War, now in 1996 celebrating the issue, right there in Talcott, of a thirty-two-cent first class John Henry stamp. The town is celebrating the first annual John Henry Days festival. It's going to put the town on the map.

Also in Talcott is Pamela Street, there to sell the town the contents of her late father's John Henry Museum, which filled her family's apartment in Harlem, a museum containing hundreds of recordings of the song, every sheet music version, lawn jockeys, paintings, theatrical programs and costumes, even five spikes a salesman claimed came from the Big Bend tunnel in Talcott, the very spot where John Henry stood side by side with the steam drill and a pistol shot sent them off. Her father bought all five—"the new school clothes could wait"—and hung them over the mantel. To a little girl they were five scary, threatening fingers: "a railroad hand," a dead man's hand, reaching out to grab her in the night. She hates everything about John Henry: her father's obsession took away her childhood. But in spite of herself, she knows everything about John Henry.

She and J. approach the Talcott John Henry: a statue of a hugely muscled black man, stripped to the waist, with a hammer in his hands. They read the plaque: "This statue was erected in 1972 by a group of people with the same determination as the one it honors—the Talcott Ruritan Club." In Whitehead's novel, every time anyone confronts the song—a folklorist in the 1920s, seeking to prove the legend true or false, a little girl on Striver's Row in Harlem in the 1950s cheating on her piano lessons with what her outraged mother calls gutter music—they are, in their own way, singing it, and so Whitehead imagines the Talcott sculptor: "The artist was forced to rely on what the story worked on his brain. He looked at the footprint left in his psyche by the steeldriver's great strides and tried to reconstruct what such a man might look like."

"You see those dents in the statue," Pamela says to J. "People come around here and use it for target practice. One time they chained the statue to a pickup and dragged it off the pedestal down the road there. Then the statue fell off and they drove off so they found it the next day just lying in the road." "Probably not much to do here on a Saturday night," says J.

This isn't merely a story. The novel is made of accumulating detail, Whitehead researching down more than a century and then imagining every setting, every character's milieu, what a room looks like, how people talk there, what they wear, what the air is like. But there are also coded, hidden details, and this—"One time they chained the statue to a pickup and dragged it off the pedestal down the road"—is one of them. It's an illustration of the twists and tangles folk songs take as they emerge from real life, live on in the imaginative life of generations of singers and dancers, and then as the songs are pulled back into real, lived life, until you can't tell the song from the events behind it and in front of it, the real from the imaginative—when you can't tell if an event caused the song or the song caused the event. Here, the tale of people chaining the statue to a pickup truck and dragging it off of its pedestal is an inescapable, folk-fictional version of an actual historical event. For a novel published in 2001, there is no way that this is not a version of the murder of James Byrd, Jr., in Jasper, Texas, on 7 June 1998.

Byrd was forty-nine and black. He was walking home from a party. Three white men in a Ford pickup, John King, Russell Brewer, and Shawn Berry, offered him a ride; he climbed in. They drove behind a store, pulled him out, beat him with a baseball bat, chained him by his ankles to the truck, and dragged him to death. When they finally dumped the body at the gate of a local black cemetery, there was no head and no right arm. Investigators determined that Byrd had tried to keep his head off the ground until the driver swerved and smashed him into a culvert. King and Brewer were both white supremacists—King had a tattoo of a black man hanging from a tree. Berry was sentenced to life; Brewer and King were sentenced to death. Brewer was executed in 2011.

In *John Henry Days*, and in history, this event can be seen—heard—as an unsinging of "John Henry," with the black man stripped of his hammer, chained to the steam drill, and pulled through the tunnel like a coal car. It's an argument that any lynching of a black American is an unsinging of "John Henry." And it's an argument that the song itself—whether called "John Henry," "The Death of John Henry," "Nine Pound Hammer," "More About John Henry," "New Railroad," or "Spike Driver Blues"—is a symbolic unsinging of any and every lynching of a black person, an affirmation of the power of a single African-American to deny and defeat the white power set against him, even if it costs him his life, but not his dignity, with the song rolling down the decades from the 1920s, when it was first recorded, taken up by Uncle Dave Macon, Mississippi John Hurt, Paul Robeson, the Monroe Brothers, Woody Guthrie, in the present day by Bruce Springsteen, the Los Angeles techno duo Snakefarm, the Boston bluegrass combo Crooked Still, and, taking John Henry from a factless past into the historical present, the British punk singer Jon Langford. Christian Marclay's "Guitar Drag," emerging out of this complex of real and imaginary situations, is another version of this version of the song.

Born in 1955 in California, raised in Switzerland, Marclay is best known for *The Clock*, first shown in 2010: his twenty-four hour, minute-by-minute video collage of clips from thousands of movies that, playing only in real time— when you enter the viewing space in a gallery or a museum at 10:13 A.M., it's 10:13 A.M. on the screen—creates a pic-

ture of an entire, mythic day. With hundreds of projects behind him, Marclay is an inveterate visual and sound artist
who has always worked with musical themes, at first taking
commercial albums and fitting them with new covers and
labels, breaking and reassembling LPs and fitting the pieces
of different records together into one that would actually play,
redesigning, deforming, and distorting every kind of musical instrument or sound equipment, even scouring cities to
photograph music-themed signs, advertisements, tattoos, and
sound holes in walls and elevators. He is an omnivorous assemblage artist drawn to destruction: everything in his work
is about taking something out of one context and putting
it into another, or recognizing the way in which an object
has lost its original, seemingly defining context and occupied
another, so that every element of a construction, or decon-
struction, begins to tell a story it never told before—but, the
feeling is, a story it always wanted to tell.

Marclay's real life as an artist began in 1977, when, attending the Massachusetts College of Art in Boston, he
found a children's Batman record in the street, run over but
still intact. It played; Marclay was drawn to the sounds made
by the tire tracks on the grooves and the dirt and gravel embedded in them. "When a record skips or pops we hear the
surface noise, we try very hard to make an abstraction of it
so it doesn't disrupt the musical flow," he said years later. "I
try to make people aware of these imperfections and accept

them as music; the recording is sort of an illusion while the scratch on the record is more real."

On the art-world edges of the New York punk scene in the early 1980s, Marclay became a club disc jockey, a turntablist with as many as eight records spinning at once, scratching back and forth between them until a new music emerged and just as quickly erased itself. He invented the Phono-guitar, allowing him to scratch, distort, and remix a phono-graph record while performing as if he were a guitarist, right down to bending the top of his body back in full guitar-hero mode. In 1983, at the Kitchen in New York, he first played "Ghost," a scary, trance-like version of Jimi Hendrix's utterly despairing "I Don't Live Today," from 1967. Nearly twenty years after his death, Hendrix remained larger than life, an unsolved mystery: "I think Jimi's gonna be remembered for centuries, just like people like Leadbelly and Lightnin' Hopkins," John Phillips of the Mamas and the Papas said in 1992. "He's really a folk hero, another John Henry." "Will I live tomorrow?/Well, I just can't say/Will I live tomorrow? /Well, I just can't say/But I know for sure/I don't live today." Marclay didn't sing those words—or he sang them in his own way. Moving the disc back and forth, he found tones in the grooves that had never been heard before. He turned words into echoes, and battered them in the air with complaints, criticisms, denials, all the sounds of distortion, until Hendrix could seem present, as a ghost presiding over the whole affair, and, as a ghost, as physically, cruelly dead as he had ever been. "Bands were being formed right and left," Marclay said in 1992. "Grab a guitar for the first time and start a band. You would get a club date before even starting rehearsals. That's how raw it was. A lot of it was bad but it didn't matter. It was the energy that mattered."

> I grabbed a turntable and used it like a guitar. *Ghost* was an homage to Jimi Hendrix. I was using a turntable-console strapped around my neck like a guitar . . . I'd play Hendrix records, scratch them bad, crush the tone arm through the grooves, and shove the thing in the amp to get feedback. I also used a wah-wah pedal. It was very loud. The portable turntable allowed me to move around and get into some Hendrix moves. What I always liked about Hendrix is the way he was pushing the limits of his instrument, looking for new sounds even if it meant burning his guitar. But *Ghost* was also dealing with the absence of the performer—the absence or death of the performer because of the recording technology. I was playing these records, going through the motions with my surrogate guitar. It was very ritualistic. I sort of became Jimi Hendrix. Instead of playing air-guitar, I was playing records.

What Marclay did onstage with "Ghost" is what he did on video with *Guitar Drag*. In 1998 he was on an airplane, reading *Time*; there was a story about the James Byrd murder. The only photo was of the back of the killers' Ford, rust covering the insides and outside of the truck, with the license plate dead center, smashed, bent, the paint scratched to the point where TEXAS was barely legible. The picture stayed in Marclay's mind as an image that wanted to be taken farther. A year later, in San Antonio as a resident artist, he determined to do it. He borrowed a truck—"from Linda Ronstadt's cousin," he said in 2013. "A Ford, a flatbed—or a Chevrolet, which has rock & roll resonance all over the place." He recruited two people to shoot from the truck bed; he scouted locations. He mounted a Trace Elliot amplifier in the back of the truck.

As the video begins, a thin man, his face obscured by a baseball cap, is holding a new Fender Stratocaster. He plugs it in; with forceful gestures, he knots a rope around its neck and secures it to the back of the truck. He gets into the driver's seat, starts the engine, and drives off. "I didn't know if it was right, as a white artist, with a race crime," Marclay said in 2013—even though, as the driver, he was throwing himself all the way into the story: he was the killer. Isaac Julien, a black British installation artist and filmmaker, was with Marclay in San Antonio: "Do it," he said.

Immediately, the guitar is jerking, turning over, every movement, every movement inside every movement, shouting out of the amplifier, and at first you are attuned to the guitar as an instrument, interested to see what kind of noise it will make, and how long it will last. There is no reference to

James Byrd. But within seconds you are drawn into the destruction as a thing in itself, an act with its own imperatives, rules, values, and aesthetics, and that destruction soon casts off any perspectives not completely sucked into an irreducible violence.

Marclay takes the truck down a paved road. Even if no thought of James Byrd enters your mind, even if you are sorting through art-world or rock 'n' roll references—"the tradition of guitar-smashing," Marclay has said of his own sense of the piece, "of the destruction of instruments in Fluxus"—the guitar is becoming a living thing, an animal or a person, something that can feel pain, and you are hearing it scream. The truck turns onto what looks like a dead swamp, a field of scrub and weeds, as if to drown the guitar in dirt. The sound it is making is full, undiminished, shooting out in too many directions. The truck races into woods, down back roads. There are constant cuts—sometimes Marclay stopped the truck and changed places with one of the videographers and vice versa—but there is no feeling of that. This is a race, a race to see how long it will take to destroy the guitar and whatever symbols and allegories, along with leaves, vines, and rocks, are wrapping themselves around the neck and tuning pegs—allegories like Dock Boggs's stalker's version of the murder ballad "Pretty Polly": "He led her over hills and valleys so deep / He led her over hills and valleys so deep / At length Pretty Polly, she begin to weep."

You are watching torture. You begin to flinch. You might turn away, but even if you don't look there's no stopping the sound. There is no abstraction. The truck pulls back onto a paved road, swerving hard to the left, to the right, the guitar swinging on the rope from one side of the road straight to the other, and while there may be a thinning in the sound, a hollowness, there's no way to anticipate when the volume will shoot up, when a sound the guitar hasn't made before will rise up and die. The truck slows down, speeds up, pulls the guitar over railroad tracks, through rocks and ever rougher surfacing, the guitar still speaking. The truck turns onto a wider road, a highway, the guitar slamming the pavement, by this time perhaps all the strings gone, the tuning pegs broken, and sound still streaming out of the body. What was clandestine before—the swamp, the field, the back roads—is now public, a crime in progress, anyone can see it, and you think, surely the police will stop it? There is no one else on the road. Is the man still in the cab of the truck? Is this some drama now so caught up in its own momentum it can play itself?

"We could not kill it," Marclay said in 2013. "We tried to: that moment when the guitar goes over the train tracks, embedded in the ground, but it still jumps into the air—the tracks marking the racial divide." As the piece ends—and you can feel it ending, slowing down—the truck crests a hill in a haze of sun and dust, like the end of a western, John

Wayne framed in the light in the cabin door in *The Search-ers*, any movie cowboy trailing off into the sunset with his horse. There is no resolution, no real ending at all. "Once you go down that road," Marclay said in 2013, echoing *De-tour* or *Raw Deal* or so many other noir films of the 1940s, "there's no way out."

Guitar Drag is a scratch in the record—the historical rec-ord. If you put the soundtrack record back on with all of this in the front of your mind, other music begins to rise out of it. There is most of all Jimi Hendrix's Woodstock trans-formation of "The Star-Spangled Banner," the greatest and most unstable protest song there is: every time you hear it, it says something else. In the twisting abstractions of that performance, in the music of *Guitar Drag*—you can't call it chance music; you could call it forced music—you can begin to hear the droning abstractions in the blues. The gonging in Blind Lemon Jefferson's 1928 "See That My Grave Is Kept Clean." The intimations of the uncanny and the unknowable in the way Robert Johnson's guitar strings seem to stand apart from his fingers in his 1936 "Come on in My Kitchen." The push toward wordlessness, into a music of pure signs, the refusal to even approach a narrative, in John Lee Hooker's "John Henry," with a pace that, if the true con-text of Hooker's song is not a private recording for a record collector in 1949 but a video by a sound artist more than half a century later, can seem to match the pacing of *Guitar*

Drag so completely that Hooker's own guitar could have been cut right into the noise made by the amplifier on the truck and the guitar on the road. "John Henry laid his hammer down / And headed back to his hometown / But someone turned the signpost round / Someone took the road signs down," Jon Langford sang in 2006 in his strongest Welsh accent in "Lost in America," a song about the American Dream as snake oil that the singer buys in spite of himself — and soon John Henry is everywhere, taking the place of the engineer in "Wreck of the Old 97" in Virginia in 1903, "Scalded to death by the dream," then, one September morning just two years short of a century after that, reappearing in the last verse to reveal Superman as merely one more version of the superman who was there first, John Henry stepping forth, once more, to "turn the planes around today / Make them fly the other way."

John Henry, the man who denied the machine, the machine that, in the Disney version of the story, comes out of the other side of the mountain as a single metal scrap, the former slave who traces his country's history in "Lost in America," is in *Guitar Drag*. "The record is supposed to be a stable reproduction of time," Marclay said in 1991, speaking of any recording, by anyone, "but it's not. Time and sound become elusive again because of mechanical failure. Technology captures sound and stamps it on these disks. They then begin lives of their own. Within these lives, technological cracks—defects—occur. That's when it gets interesting for me, when technology fails. That's when I feel the possibility of expression." Isn't that what John Henry says, when he challenges the steam drill to a duel?

You can hear the heedlessness of "Shake Some Action" in *Guitar Drag*; you can hear Little Richard's "Keep A Knockin'." I imagine Little Richard alone in the setting Marclay designed for viewings of *Guitar Drag*—"a projection, it has to be loud, it has to be experienced in a black box where you can lose track of time and space, lose your balance. The image is jerky and you may get dizzy. It has to be a physical experience you need to feel it through your body"—and I imagine Little Richard tapping his foot. I think of the end of *American Hot Wax*.

In this 1978 movie, it's 1959. Tim McIntire's Alan Freed arrives outside the Brooklyn Paramount for his big rock 'n' roll extravaganza, with Chuck Berry and Jerry Lee Lewis topping the bill—appearing in the movie as themselves, Berry time-traveling effortlessly, Lewis making it by sheer force of will. There's a huge crowd outside. As Freed heads for the entrance, standing straight, moving to his own beat, snapping his limbs like fingers, he's accosted by a Dion figure. He's got this group, Mr. Freed, he wants to audition right on the street; Freed calls for quiet and they go right into an acappella "I Wonder Why." Freed's grin is tight, hinting at fear, fatalism, even suicide. His career is crashing all around him. He's about to be kicked off the air, blacklisted for payola; the D.A. is going to shut down his show and throw him in jail. McIntire, like Freed an alcoholic, a drug addict, carried all that with him, dying at forty-one, eight years after playing Freed, who died at forty-three: "Dead frequency, Slick, over and out," Charles Wright wrote of McIntire in 2005. "It's mostly a matter of what kind of noise you make."

Through the window of the D.A.'s car, hovering on the edges of the crowd, you see a ragged figure, in a state of utter obliviousness, pounding on an overturned garbage can, his pompadour flopping into his face, shouting out "Good Golly Miss Molly" so tunelessly you can barely recognize it. This is less Little Richard not invited to the Brooklyn Paramount but showing up anyway than it's the Little Richard specter—the specter of the excluded, silenced, worthless music hovering behind every finished piece of rock 'n' roll, the unheard music that reveals the music that is heard as a fake. In his car, plotting strategy, the D.A. doesn't notice the bum in the alley, he isn't listening to him, but subconsciously he hears him, and what he hears is what he sees. "Look at that filth," the D.A. says of the boys and girls, black and white, crowding into the theater.

With Jerry Lee Lewis as the last act, standing on top of his burning piano and the stage covered with cops, teenagers grabbed by police as others are trampled as they rush down the stairs, the audience flees into the night. Freed clutches a small boy. In the last shot, the bum stands on the now-deserted street, playing for the sky, pounding his can: "I say a wop bop a loo bop a lop bam boom. Got a girl. Named Sue. She knows just what to do. Got a girl"—and the movie is over. That scene too is in the music of *Guitar Drag*.

To Know Him Is to Love Him

1958·2006

In 1958, the Teddy Bears released "To Know Him Is to Love Him," a number 1 hit written by Teddy Bear Phil Spector, a song that took forty-eight years to find its voice. When Amy Winehouse sang it in 2006, her music curled around Spector's, his curled around her, until she found her way back to the beginning of his career, and redeemed it. Whether he has ever heard what she did with his music, or whether she ever heard what he thought of what she did, are unanswered questions. He isn't talking; she can't.

Since 2009, when he was convicted of second-degree murder in the 2003 shooting death of the nightclub hostess, unsuccessful actress, and sometime blackface Little Richard impersonator Lana Clarkson at his mansion in Alhambra, California, Phil Spector has been serving nineteen years to life at a division of Corcoran State Prison. Amy Winehouse has been dead since 2011. If you listen to the Teddy Bears' record now, and ignore what Spector did with the rest of his life, or even what he did in the few years after he made "To Know Him Is to Love Him," his fate may not seem like such a tragedy. If you listen to Winehouse sing the song, you can hate her for what, as over a few July days she drank herself to death, she withheld from the world.

Phil Spector was born in the Bronx in 1939; his father, the son of a Russian Jewish immigrant and a failing businessman, killed himself ten years later. In 1953 Spector's mother moved herself and her son to Los Angeles. At Fairfax High School—where only a few years before the would-be songwriter Jerry Leiber was sketching out his first rhythm and blues lyrics—Spector fell in with other students in love with the doo-wop sound in the air of the town: with the Penguins' rough, inspiring "Earth Angel," Arthur Lee Maye and the Crowns' complex and surging "Gloria," the Robins' comic operas "Framed" and "Riot in Cell Block #9," written and produced by Leiber and his partner Mike Stoller, a hundred more. Among Spector's classmates were Marshall Leib, a singer; Steve Douglas, who would go on to play saxophone on dozens of Los Angeles hits, most unforgettably Spector's 1963 production of Darlene Love's "Christmas (Baby Please Come Home)," a record so spectacular that for years Love has appeared every Christmas season on the David Letterman show to re-create it, and succeeds; and Sandy Nelson, a drummer, who in 1959 would make the top ten with "Teen Beat" and in 1961 with "Let There Be Drums," though in 1964 "Teen Beat '65" reached only number 44, and in 1965 "Let There Be Drums '66" disappeared at number 120. Spector met Lou Adler, a would-be songwriter at Roosevelt High (with Sam Cooke and Herb Alpert, he would write "Wonderful World," which Cooke made into as perfect a record as rock 'n' roll ever wished for), and Bruce Johnston, who turned up a few years later in the Beach Boys.

All of them were listening to the records coming out of other high schools, on Dootsie Williams's DooTone label or Art Rupe's Specialty. Out of Jefferson High and the half-black, half-white Fremont High, where every other person seemed to be in a group, came the Penguins, Richard Berry, who passed through many groups before making "Louie Louie" with the Pharaohs, Cornelius Gunter of the Coasters, Jesse Belvin, who co-wrote "Earth Angel" when he wasn't singing on half the sessions in the city, or maybe when he was, and Don Julian and the Meadowlarks, with their lovely, ridiculous "Heaven and Paradise." From different schools in Compton and Watts there came the Medallions' even more ridiculous "The Letter," which leader Vernon Green didn't seem to know was ridiculous at all: "Let me whisper," he declaimed, as if he were in a school play delivering Romeo's plea to Juliet on her balcony but got lost, "sweet words, of dismortality, and discuss, the pompitus of love. Put it together, and what do you have? *Matrimony!*" "There used to be hundreds and hundreds of black groups singin' harmony and with a great lead singer," Spector said years later. "You used to go down to Jefferson High on 49th and Broadway and could get sixteen groups." All over town, Spector and the rest sang the songs together until they got them right. They wrote their own songs.

Spector wrote "To Know Him Is to Love Him." Along with Leib and Annette Kleinbard, another Fairfax classmate, he formed the Teddy Bears. They made a demo, got a contract with the local label Era. With Kleinbard singing lead, Spector playing guitar and along with Leib singing the backing "And I do and I do and I do"s behind the verses and the "Oom-da-da Oom da-da"s on the bridge, Sandy Nelson playing all but inaudible drums, and Spector, the eighteen-year-old producer, layering the voices over each other, they made a record. Within months the tune was at the top of the charts all over the country. The Teddy Bears lip-synched it on Dick Clark's *American Bandstand*, the national after-noon show from Philadelphia that served as a living juke-box for rock 'n' roll, the ultimate showcase. No, it wasn't as prestigious as the *Ed Sullivan Show*, and Elvis Presley never appeared on *American Bandstand*, but even with singers and musicians just miming their records, the show carried a greater sense of risk. Will they—the kids dancing on the show, the kids glued to their TV sets, the kids talking about it the next day at school—like it? Will they laugh? Klein-bard was in the middle, in a white prom dress and short dark hair. Leib and Spector flanked her in pale prom tuxes, Leib tall, dark, handsome, broad-shouldered, Spector short, his chin weak, his shoulders tense and cramped: an undis-guisable high-school nerd, under his pompadour obviously already losing his hair, his thin tenor pulling away from his own song as if he were afraid of his own voice. All his life, he never stopped telling people where the song came from:

"I took it from the words on my father's grave." "'I took it from the words on my grave,'" he said in the early 1970s to Nik Cohn, who was in Los Angeles to write a book with him about his life. "He was standing at the window, looking down at the Strip," Cohn wrote later. "For a few seconds he noticed nothing. Just stood there, this tiny, ancient child, with his hair all wisps and his shades refracting silver. Then he heard what he'd said and he turned to face me. He did not look distressed; just puzzled, lost. 'Not my grave. I meant my father's,' he said. 'The words on my father's grave.'"

Despite a nice, swaying rhythm, and a comforting melody not that far from Leonard Cohen's "Hallelujah," the closest a mere song has ever come to sainthood, the record was weak—it all but worshiped weakness, advertised it as a way of life. It made all too much sense that, in another story Spector could never stop telling, one night in Philadelphia, in 1958, in the backstage men's room after he'd performed with the Teddy Bears on a bill with a dozen other acts, four guys pulled knives, pushed him into a men's room stall, told him to sit down, slowly unbuttoned their jeans, and pissed all over him. I heard him tell the story to a full hall at Berkeley in 1966, when his career as the most envied record producer in the world—for the Crystals' "He's a Rebel" and "Da Doo Ron Ron," Darlene Love's "(Today I Met) The Boy I'm Gonna Marry" and "Fine, Fine Boy," the Ronettes' "Be My Baby" and "Walking in the Rain," the Righteous Brothers' "You've

Lost that Lovin' Feeling," and a full Top 40's worth more from 1961 to 1966—seemed over, at least to Spector himself. Ike and Tina Turner's "River Deep-Mountain High," his most ambitious record, with the biggest, most implacable sound and an arrangement that made it feel as if the record lasted a lifetime, not three and a half minutes ("That," the Grateful Dead guitarist Jerry Garcia said, "sounds like God hit the world and the world hit back"), failed to come anywhere near the radio; Spector closed his studio and began lecturing at colleges. "I didn't really know what was going on," he said of that night backstage. "I thought it was some kind of initiation, you know, like after it was all over they were going to let me into their club"—he told the story without embarrassment, without shame, as if it were funny, just one of those things, he was explaining, along with rigged contracts, third-party lawsuits, phony promoters, and electric fences, that rock 'n' roll was really about, as if he would never get over it.

After the novelty wore off, after the radio wore the song out, "To Know Him Is to Love Him" stood simpering, dripping treacle, almost crossing the line from sentimental homily to prayer, a dirge at its most lifelike. It was music far behind rock 'n' roll, music for weddings without dancing, too square for proms, like the material the Teddy Bears used to fill out their only album: "Unchained Melody" and "Tammy." Spector had to know the song was a dead fish; in the years to come he never tried to pawn it off on any of the performers on his own Philles label, not even the hopeless Bob B. Soxx of the Blue Jeans.

Amy Winehouse was born in London in 1983. "I'm Russian Jew," she once said bluntly: she learned to sing, she said, from listening to Mahalia Jackson, Dinah Washington, Ray Charles, and Thelonious Monk. It was only in her early twenties that she was captured by Spector's female singers, by "Tonight's the Night," "Will You Love Me Tomorrow," and other shimmering singles by the Shirelles, and most of all by the Shangri-Las. They were two sets of sisters from Andrew Jackson High in Queens, New York.

The Shangri-Las' producer and songwriter was George "Shadow" Morton, twenty-four. One day in 1964, as he always told the story, he showed up at 1650 Broadway, having heard that his old friend Ellie Greenwich was writing songs there; he met her husband and songwriting partner, Jeff Barry. "He turned to me," Morton recalled in 2001 for a TV documentary, the barest hint of a grin curling at the corners of his mouth, letting you see his eyes twinkling behind his shades, "and said, 'Well, just what is it you do for a living?' 'Well,' I said, 'actually, some people would call it being a bum, but I'm a songwriter, just like you.' So he said, 'What kind of songs do you write?' And I said, 'Hit songs.' And he said, 'Why don't you bring one in and show it to us?' And I said, 'You've got to tell me: you want a fast hit or a slow hit?'

He said, 'Make it slow.' And on the way to the studio, I realized, I didn't have a—I didn't have a song. I had ideas, but—
so I pulled the car over, on a place called South Oyster Bay
Road, and I wrote a song." It was "Remember (Walking in
the Sand)," the first of three top ten hits by the Shangri-
Las on Red Bird Records, the independent New York label
formed in 1964 by Leiber, Stoller, and George Goldner. "It
was very corny," Leiber said thirty-seven years later of the
song Morton brought in. "Very sweet, and, finally, somewhere, touching. It wasn't synthetic. It was for real—like he
was."

The record was melodramatic, distant, dark, hard to catch,
moving the way you walk in the sand, the ground slipping
under your feet. It began with heavy bass notes on a piano,
reached past itself with the faraway cawing of seagulls, a
sardonic chorus of ghosts snapping fingers, and harsh, cold
voices chanting "*Remember*," as if the singer telling the story
could ever forget. On paper it was about a boy telling a girl
they were through; on record, like all of the Shangri-Las'
best records, it was about death. The cadence was blunt,
broken, stark.

> What will happen to
> The life I gave to you?
> What will I do with it now?

With anyone but sixteen-year-old Mary Weiss as the lead singer, the unrelieved doom in the music might have turned into a joke, but it never happened, not in "Remember," "Give Us Your Blessings," "Out in the Streets," "Past, Present, and Future," or "I Can Never Go Home Anymore," not even in the comic-strip play "Leader of the Pack." "I had enough pain in me, at the time," Weiss said in 2001, "to pull off anything. And to get into it, and sound—believable. It was very easy for me," she said with a big, thank-God-that's-behind-me smile. "The recording studio was the place that you could really release what you're feeling, without everybody looking at you." In 2001, Weiss was working for a New York furniture company; on September 11 she was downtown, a few blocks north of the World Trade Center. She saw the first plane hit, then the second. Two weeks later, ending an essay she wrote about the event, she fell back into the hard count of "Remember," as if the pacing of the song, like the others she sang, had long since for her become a language, a way to speak about what you couldn't speak about, a way of placing yourself in the world: "New York will never be the same. The United States will never be the same. For that matter I will never be the same person.

"We all want to go to sleep, and wake up and realize it's been a bad dream.

"It's not."

That was the language Amy Winehouse heard. It was a language she learned. The Shangri-Las' records became talismans, charms, fetish objects, voodoo dolls signifying curses she laid on herself. "I didn't want to just wake up drinking, and crying, and listening to the Shangri-Las, and go to sleep, and wake up drinking, and listening to the Shangri-Las," Winehouse would say of how she wrote her unflinching songs, but she did. That was why, over and over again onstage, she would let "Remember" drift in and out of the almost sickeningly deliberate pace of "Back to Black," the title song of her second album, released in 2006, and her last while she was alive, until you had to hear the two songs as one. That was why, in her irresistible, unreadable 2008 Grammy performance of "You Know I'm No Good"—via a live hookup from London; Winehouse's drug addiction kept her out of the United States—Winehouse was her own leader of the pack, but without a pack, without the girlfriends Mary Weiss had around her to ask her if she was really going out with him, if she was really going all the way, if she was really ready to throw her life in the gutter. Winehouse might not have had anything on her side but the satisfaction of getting it right, saying what she had to say, adding something to the form that had brought her to life as an artist, adding her name and face and the story it told. Yes, she wrote "You Know I'm No Good," and like any work of art it was a fiction that bounced back on real life, maybe the author's, maybe not; as she sang the song on the Grammys, you could hear and see her listening to the song as well as singing it, hear the song talking to her, hear her asking herself, as she sang, *Is that true? Is that what I want? Is that who I am? Is that all I've got?*

One day in 2006 Winehouse stepped to the microphone in a BBC disc jockey's studio to sing "To Know Him Is to Love Him," and with a guitarist softly fingering doo-wop triplets, a drummer tapping, and a bassist counting off notes as if he'd thought about each one, she unlocked the song. In the three seconds it took her to climb through the first five words, to sing "To know, know, know him," you were in a different country than any the song had ever reached before. All of Winehouse's commitment to the songwriter's craft, the way her professionalism was inseparable from her fandom, was brought to bear as she sang; it also disappeared, leaving both her and the song in limbo, out of time, no need to go forward, no need to go back. With the slightly acrid scratch that sometimes crept into her harder songs dissolved in a creamy vortex, the feeling was scary, and delicious; in those three seconds, then moving on through the first lines with hesitations between words and syllables so rich with the specter of someone facing the Spector tombstone and reading the words off of it out loud, TO KNOW HIM WAS TO LOVE HIM, each word as she sang it demanding the right to be the last word, or merely wishing for it, the song expanded as if, all those years, it had been waiting for this particular singer to be born, and was only now letting out its breath. You could tell, listening, that Winehouse had worked on the song for a long time. "Congratulations!" said the disc jockey, Pete Mitchell, when the performance was over. "Recorded by the Teddy Bears!" "It's like when somebody dies—all the people do is yell 'He died, he died,'" Phil Spector said in 1969. "I yell 'He lived.' A hell of a lot more important than the fact that he's dead, is the fact that he lived."

"She could not stand fame any more than I could," Mary Weiss said in 2011, after Winehouse was found dead in her London house, after the torrent of her-whole-life-was-a-train-wreck, anyone-could-have-seen-it-coming schaden-freude that followed. "I related to her so much it is a bit scary. I will never understand why people get off kicking people when they are down and need help. How could that possibly make you feel better about yourself?"

"I was asking her to be an actress, not just a singer," Morton said of Weiss. Her songs, like Winehouse's, were all locked doors, doors that locked you out or that you locked yourself from the inside. But maybe because Weiss can still speak plainly—"I wish I could have helped her, even if she never sang publically again," Weiss said—inside her words one can perhaps see other lives for Amy Winehouse: a junkie on the street like Marianne Faithfull, who finally walked away, back into the career she never really had the first time around, first recording in the same year the Shangri-Las first recorded, in 2011 covering their "Past, Present, and Future" on a new album; a music teacher for kindergarteners; a grimy singer with a guitar case open at her feet, like anyone in your town; an old woman with stories nobody believes. Like Shadow Morton, with the demeanor of a born hipster, Mohair Sam himself, telling his stories, thinking about how, in 1966, with George Goldner's mob gambling debts hanging over the company, Leiber and Stoller sold it for a dollar and got out of town. "The girls in the Shangri-Las," he said, "they became the Shadowesses. I mean, they disappeared, they *vacated*. And a lot of the other girls who were with Red Bird, they just seemed to—like dust. As if it never was." But what did he know? That was only one version of the story, and there is an infinity of stories that tell this tale.

Notes

A NEW LANGUAGE

Allen Ruppersberg, *Collector's Paradise* (New York: Christine Burgin, 2013), unpaginated. Published in conjunction with the Ruppersberg exhibition "No Time Left to Start Again / The B (birth) and D (death) of R 'n' R," the Art Institute of Chicago, 21 September 2012–6 January 2013. "I chose to stop the collection in the period of the early 1970s, as it seems to me, as it does to many others, that at about that time rock and roll was becoming something other than its original self. The spark of invention that was once so new and exciting had begun to change into something we now call rock. Some would date the demise to the death of Elvis Presley. I just stopped a little earlier. It was reinvented in the late 1970s with the birth of punk but that's someone else's story."

Nik Cohn, *Pop from the Beginning* (London: Weidenfeld and Nicholson, 1969), published in the United States as *Rock from the Beginning* (New York: Stein and Day, 1969); revised as *Awopbopaloobop Alopbamboom* (London: Paladin, 1972).

Jim Miller, ed., *The Rolling Stone Illustrated History of Rock & Roll*, rev. ed. (1976; New York: Rolling Stone/Random House, 1980). The 1992 edition, with editorial credit to Anthony De-

Curtis, Jim Henke, and Holly George-Warren, is not recommended.

Guy Peellaert and Nik Cohn, *Rock Dreams* (New York: Rogner and Bernhard, 1982).

"Yahweh came down": Genesis 11:5, as translated by David Rosenberg in Harold Bloom, *The Book of J* (New York: Grove Weidenfeld, 1990), 53.

Colin B. Morton (Carlton B. Morgan) and Chuck Death (Jon Langford), "Bobby Dylan Part 2," *Great Pop Things*, collected in *Great Pop Things* (London: Penguin, 1992; expanded ed. Portland, Ore.: Verse Chorus Press, 1998), 31 in the U.S. ed. *Great Pop Things* began as a weekly strip in the U.K. in 1987, in *Record Mirror* and the *New Musical Express*, continued at *LA Weekly* and *New City* (Chicago), and ceased regular publication in 1998, though it still pops up here and there.

Pete Townshend quoted in Jann Wenner, "The Rolling Stone Interview," *Rolling Stone*, 14 September 1968, 15.

Bob Dylan, "It's Alright, Ma (I'm Only Bleeding)," from *Bringing It All Back Home* (Columbia, 1965), in "Made in America," *The Sopranos*, written and directed by David Chase (HBO, 10 June 2007).

Dennis Potter quoted in Michael Sragow, "BBC Pro Shows ABC's of Dream Writing," *San Francisco Sunday Examiner and Chronicle*, 29 March 1987. In his musicals, people don't just break into song. Old songs descend on them like visitations. The original recordings come out of the characters' mouths and change them. The actors are mouthing the words, but it feels not as if something is being faked but as if something real but previously unknown is being revealed; the songs work as subconscious dialogue. "It became a technical problem for me," Potter said in 1994 to the BBC TV host Melvyn Bragg, two months before he died. "It was about how do I get that music from way down there, bang up in front. And then I thought they lip-synch things. I wasn't breaking a mold, I found the ideal way of making these songs real." See "Living for the Present: Dennis Potter's Last Interview," *Guardian*, 6 April 1994.

David Lynch, in Chris Rodley, *Lynch on Lynch: Revised Edition* (London: Faber and Faber, 2005), 126–27.

W. T. Lhamon, Jr., *Deliberate Speed: The Origins of a Cultural Style in the American 1950s* (Washington, D.C.: Smithsonian Institution Press, 1990), 93. "Their performance," Lhamon writes of the people making "Tutti Frutti" in 1955, "took on a licentious exuberance commensurate to their release from restraint. Having found a strategy for eluding the censors, public and private, their speed and joy in the song memorialize both their freedom and the trick the song pulls off: ramming its underground reality to the mainstream airwaves. This is the quintessence of the sort of complex Samboing Little Richard enacted."

Richard Nevins, Dick Spottswood, and Pete Whelan, "Recollections," liner notes to *The Return of the Stuff that Dreams Are Made Of* (Yazoo, 2012). "A collection of 46 classics of American traditional music recorded in the 1920s," including Uncle Dave Macon and His Fruit Jar Drinkers' 1927 "Sail Away Ladies" (Nevins: "with no hesitation or qualification whatsoever the greatest record of all time . . . No other record has ever combined in one performance such high degrees of joyous celebration, uninhibited exuberance, motive expressiveness [especially in the tune's transcendent high part], pure power, and infectious rhythm"), Allison's Sacred Harp Singers' "I'm a Long Time Traveling Away from Home," also 1927, Henry Thomas's 1929 "Charmin' Betsy," and Geeshie Wiley's 1930 "Last Kind Words Blues."

"SHAKE SOME ACTION" 1976

Neil Young and Bill Flanagan, in Flanagan, *Written in My Soul: Conversations with Rock's Greatest Songwriters* (Chicago: Contemporary Books, 1986), 128–29.

"I really try"; "You have to go into a crowd": Neil Young to GM, in "Neil Young," *Spin*, January 1994, 35, 34.

Handsome Family, "Winnebago Skeletons," from *Milk and Scissors* (Carrot Top, 1996).

Flamin' Groovies, "Shake Some Action," on *Shake Some Action* (Sire, 1976). Produced by Dave Edmunds at Rockfield in 1972.

Cyril Jordan quoted in notes by Michael Goldberg and Michael Snyder for *Groovies Greatest Grooves* (Sire, 1989).

Kill Rock Stars (Kill Rock Stars, 1991). With early, sometimes first recordings by Bratmobile ("Girl Germs"), Courtney Love ("Don't Mix the Colors"), Nirvana ("Beeswax"), Bikini Kill ("Feels Blind"), 7 Year Bitch ("8-Ball Deluxe"), the Melvins ("Ever Since My Accident"), and Heavens to Betsy ("My Red Self").

"TRANSMISSION" 2007 / 1979 / 2010

Control, directed by Anton Corbijn, written by Matt Greenhalgh (Three Dogs and a Pony, 2007). The version of "Transmission" as performed by the actors is included on *Control—Music from the Motion Picture* (Warner Bros., 2007).

Elvis Costello, "Radio Radio" (Radar, 1978).

"God, what the fuck"; "Some nights"; "Now, finally, he understood": Anthony Wilson, *24 Hour Party People—What the Sleeve
Notes Never Tell You* (London: Channel 4, 2002), 24–25, 81, 49. A
third-person memoir, the book is presented as a novelization of
the movie of the same name, which chronicled Wilson's career
in Manchester—television host, founder of the Factory label, creator of the Hacienda, the twentieth-century European avant-garde
boiled down into a single nightclub. Born in 1950, he died in 2007.

Joy Division, a documentary film directed by Grant Gee and
written by Jon Savage (Hudson Productions, 2007). Some quotes
from Bernard Sumner ("'Yeah Yeah,'" "The words"), Peter Hook
("We were doing"), and Tony Wilson "("Punk was") come from
this source.

"None of us"; "I always felt"; "When you play it": Peter Hook to
GM, 31 January 2013.

Leslie Fiedler, Introduction to *No! In Thunder: Essays on Myth
and Literature* (1960), in *The Collected Essays of Leslie Fiedler*,
vol. 1 (New York: Stein and Day, 1971), 237–38.

Jon Savage, "Joy Division: 'Unknown Pleasures,'" *Melody
Maker*, 21 July 1979.
——— "good evening, we're joy division": notes to Joy Division, *Heart and Soul*, a four-CD collection of released and unreleased studio recordings and live recordings (London, 1997).
Some quotes from Bernard Sumner ("It was because," "He was
Ian") come from this superb essay.

Albert Camus, "What do you think of American literature?
'Literature of the basic,' Answers Albert Camus," interview with
Jean Desternes, *Combat*, 17 January 1947, collected in *Camus at
Combat—Writing, 1944–1947*, ed. Jacqueline Lévi-Valensi, trans.

Arthur Goldhammer (Princeton: Princeton University Press, 2006), 279.

Joy Division, *Unknown Pleasures* (Factory, 1979). Collected on *Heart and Soul,* as above, as are other Joy Division recordings mentioned unless otherwise referenced.

—— "Transmission," March 1979 Genetic Records demo.

—— "Transmission" (Factory, October 1979).

—— "The Factory, Manchester—Live 13 July 1979," included on reissue of *Unknown Pleasures* (London/Rhino, 2007).

—— "Transmission," for John Peel's *Something Else,* 1 September 1979, collected on *The Complete BBC Recordings* (True North, 2000); footage can be seen in the documentary *Joy Division,* above. In *Control,* "Transmission" as introduced by Tony Wilson is based on this performance, though when Joy Division actually appeared on Wilson's *Granada Reports,* they played "Shadowplay."

Graham Greene, *Brighton Rock* (1938; London: Compact, 1993), 218–20. In *The Sex Pistols* (London: Universal, 1978), Fred and Judy Vermorel suggest that Johnny Rotten derived his punk persona partly from Greene's Pinkie.

Brighton Rock, directed by John Boulting, written by Graham Greene and Terence Rattigan (Associated British Picture Corporation, 1947).

Brighton Rock, written and directed by Rowan Joffe (Studio Canal, 2010).

"Crime Leaders Kray Twins Schemed to Take Over as the Beatles' Managers," TopNews.in, 21 June 2009.

Paul McCartney quoted from Anthony Wall's heartbreaking two-and-a-half-hour documentary *The Brian Epstein Story* (BBC

Arena, 1998, produced by Debbie Geller) and Debbie Geller's oral biography *In My Life: The Brian Epstein Story*, ed. Anthony Wall (New York: Thomas Dunne/St. Martin's, 2000), 138.

"IN THE STILL OF THE NITE" 1956 / 1959 / 2010

Five Satins, "In the Still of the Nite" (Standord/Ember, 1956, number 24; 1960, number 81; 1961, number 99).

Oldies But Goodies (Original Sound, 1959). Also included on the first, "Dreamy" side, were the Penguins' 1954 "Earth Angel," the Teen Queens' 1956 "Eddie My Love," the Mello Kings' 1957 "Tonite Tonite," Don Julian & the Meadowlarks' 1955 "Heaven and Paradise," and the Medallions' 1954 "The Letter"—all from Los Angeles.

Fred Parris and Vinny Mazzetta quoted in Randall Beach, "Vinny Played Sax. The Five Satins Needed a Solo. The Rest Was History," *New Haven Register*, 5 December 2010.

"What's interesting": Robert Ray to GM, 1992.

Dead Ringers, directed by David Cronenberg, written by Cronenberg and Norman Snider (Morgan Creek, 1988).

Slades, "You Cheated" (Domino, 1958, number 42). See *The Domino Records Story* (Ace, 1998), which includes "You Gambled," "I Cheated," and the Slades' rehearsal tapes, and also Ed Ward on Domino Records, *Fresh Air*, WHYY, 3 September 2002.

Shields, "You Cheated" (Tender/Dot, 1958, number 12).

"Jesse'd write these songs": Gaynel Hodge quoted in Jim Dawson's notes to Jesse Belvin, *"Hang Your Tears Out to Dry"* (Earth Angel, 1986), a collection that includes recordings from 1951 to 1957, though not the tune for which Belvin is best known, "Good-night My Love (Pleasant Dreams)," from 1956—and covered in 2012 by Aaron Neville on *My True Story* (Blue Note) with a touch so light it betrays the fear that to press down any harder on the song would be to shatter it.

Ronnie Hawkins, "You Cheated (You Lied)," on *Mr. Dynamo* (Roulette, 1960). Roulette was owned by Morris Levy, long a front for the Genovese crime family; song stealing was all but automatic. Levon Helm, in 1960 an unknowing sub-sub-sub-front for the Genovese crime family, was still credited as the author of "You Cheated" on a 1994 Ronnie Hawkins reissue, which meant Roulette, or the Genovese crime family, was still collecting royalties from it.

Safaris, "Image of a Girl" (Eldo, 1960, number 6).

Geeshie Wiley, "Last Kind Words Blues" (Paramount, 1930). See *American Primitive, Vol. II: Pre-War Revenants, 1897–1939* (Revenant, 2005).

John Jurgensen, "Should Bob Dylan Retire?" *Wall Street Journal*, 2 December 2010.

"ALL I COULD DO WAS CRY"   2013 / 1960 / 2008

George Packer, "Loose Thoughts on Youth and Age," *New Yorker* Daily Comment, 8 February 2013.

The Jerk, directed by Carl Reiner, written by Steve Martin, Carl Gottlieb, and Micael Elias (Universal, 1979).

Rick Perlstein, "The Long Con: Mail-Order Conservatism," *Baffler*, no. 21, Fall 2012.

Etta James and "The Peaches," "The Wallflower (Roll with Me Henry)" or "Dance with Me Henry" (Modern, 1955).

Etta James, "All I Could Do Was Cry" (Argo, 1960).

—— "At Last" (Argo, 1961).

"I liked to see"; "The song has me": Etta James and David Ritz, *A Rage to Survive: The Etta James Story* (New York: Da Capo, 2003), 108, 96.

John Fahey, *How Bluegrass Music Destroyed My Life* (Chicago: Drag City, 2000).

James Agee, "Comedy's Greatest Era," *Life*, 3 September 1949, collected in Agee, *Film Writing and Selected Journalism* (New York: Library of America, 2005), 19.

"She is going to have a hill to climb": Etta James quoted on Page 6 of the *New York Post*, so who knows. Quoted by Kenyon Farrow in "A Political Obituary for Etta James," *Color Lines*, 24 January 2012.

Cadillac Records, written and directed by Darnell Martin (Tri-Star, 2008). Beyoncé is the only reason to see it—and unfortunately it cornered the market. Another film on Chess Records was in production at the same time; when it finally appeared, in 2010, its release was indistinguishable from its disappearance.

Cadillac Records never thinks beyond biography. *Who Do You Love*, directed by Jerry Zaks, written by Peter Wortman and Robert Conte, exposes the falsity of the biopic, where a putatively tragic or redemptive story is imposed on the various events in a life as if they were heading to the preordained end the script has imposed: in other words, always engaged in a circular argument with itself, the biopic is a snake eating its own tail. Instead of a concrete story, *Who Do You Love* has a theme—a theme that carries its characters through the years, without any resolution at all.

It begins in Chicago in 1933, when two boys hear country blues for the first time, played by a bum on the street. "My man," he says to Leonard and Phil Chess, sixteen and twelve, though they look much younger. "My *man*," says Leonard, leaning down to slap the man's hand. He looks down into the man's upside-down hat, with two small coins in it. "Slow day," says the man. Leonard searches his pockets and comes up empty. "Don't worry," he says, taking out a pencil and a piece of paper and scribbling on his brother's back for a desk. "What's that?" says the man. "That's my IOU. I owe you five cents." "Well," says the man, "ain't that a motherfucker." We follow the boys onto a streetcar, then into their father's salvage yard. "You okay, motherfucker?" Len says. "I'm okay, motherfucker," Phil says, trying to look tough. "Me too, motherfucker," Len says. "What does this mean?" Phil asks, waking up from himself. "'Motherfucker,'" Len says, considering the question, all but holding the word up to the light: he's the older brother, he can't admit he has no idea what it means. "I think it means some kind of—" and then their father shows up. "Where have you been?" he says in a heavy Polish accent. "You think there's no work to do? A poor Jew," he says in Polish, "has to work harder."

The movie is about Leonard Chess's lifelong struggle to figure out what motherfucker means. People try to tell him—first Muddy Waters, finally Bo Diddley, who in this movie, which after the prelude goes only from 1947 to 1955, a chamber piece compared to *Cadillac Records,* is the last artist we meet—but the secret always eludes him. As Len Chess, Alessandro Nivola is slick, impulsive, daring, his eyes always burning; as the songwriter and bassist Willie Dixon, Chi McBride is the watchman, a huge man with a Cheshire cat smile, always casting a dubious eye as he sees through one moment into the next; David Oyelowo's Muddy

Waters is part minstrel trickster, part struggling businessman, but most of all a well of pride and dignity: "You know that don't do me no good," he says without embarrassment when McBride hands him a sheet of lyrics for what turns out to be "Hoochie Koochie Man." ("Does that mean what I think it does?" Chess says.) Playing the Etta James character, here a junkie named Ivy Mills who Len Chess falls for as if she were a well, who can't sing on stage or get through two lines in a studio, Megalyn Ann Echikunwoke is almost too beautiful to look at, especially when you don't expect her to live through another scene. "'Gift of God,'" she says mockingly of her voice, sitting across from Chess in a restaurant. "I can sing better when I'm all doped up. What kind of gift is that? 'Sometimes I feel like a motherless child,'" she sings, part Billie Holiday, part Dinah Washington, mostly a dream singer who never was, and here the words are a suicide note, and they come out of her like foam.

The movie is one long gasp, the humor snapping, pain unforgettable and unredeemed, its theme never pressed, merely returning like Rumpelstiltskin. Chess plays a game with every musician he hires: he sits across from him, asks him what he thinks he's worth, writes a number on a piece of paper, rips it off a pad, then hands the pad across the table. "My number or less, yes," he says, but one penny more, no. The musician invariably writes something down, Chess stares at him; he crosses out his number and writes down a lower one. "That's fucked up," says one man. "Did it with me, I'm still here," says Willie Dixon. "What he pay you for, anyway?" says the musician. "Dix is my mentor," says Chess. "Your *what?*" "I am his guide," Dixon says like a Sphinx, "into the exotic Negro world"—and, finally, Dixon will explain what motherfucker means. Late in the film, Bo Diddley sits down for his contract negotiation—and snatches Chess's piece of paper out of his hand. Dixon is thrilled. "All these years I been working with y'all I ain't never seen nobody do that, let me shake this man's hand." He looks at the slip. It's blank, and Chess changes before his eyes. "You know," Dixon says, "this is the first time I ever look at you and see a white man. I guess that makes me the dumb nigger"—and with that Chess disappears from what he thought was his story, and the book closes behind him. You want to know what a motherfucker is? Look in my eyes, motherfucker.

Phil Spector quoted in "George Goldner Dies in His Sleep at Age 52 in New York," *Rolling Stone*, 28 May 1970, 9.

Langdon Winner, "The Chantels," *Rolling Stone*, 1 November 1969, 41.

"CRYING, WAITING, HOPING" 1959 / 1969

Buddy Holly, *Not Fade Away: The Complete Studio Recordings and More* (HIP-O Select, 2009). Covering 1949 to 1968, a superbly compiled and annotated six-CD collection, from Holly's first and final home recordings to posthumous overdubs.

Bobby Vee, "To me," to GM, 1970. In 2004, Bob Dylan described his brief days in Vee's band the Shadows in 1959, and going to see him in the early '60s at the Brooklyn Paramount with "The Shirelles, Danny and the Juniors, Jackie Wilson, Ben E. King, Maxine Brown . . . He was on the top of the heap now." After the show they talked: "I told him I was playing the folk clubs, but it was impossible to give him any indication of what it was all about. His only reference would have been The Kingston Trio, Brothers Four, stuff like that. He'd become a crowd pleaser in the pop world . . . I wouldn't see Bobby Vee again for thirty years, and though things would be a lot different, I'd always thought of him as a brother. Every time I'd hear his name somewhere, it was like he was in the room." *Chronicles, Volume One* (New York: Simon and Schuster, 2004), 80–81. On 10 July 2013, on tour in St. Paul, with Vee in the crowd, Dylan played "Suzie Baby," Vee's first record, from 1959, a song he'd written in Buddy Holly's style, and both as a song and a performance it was perfect, a body made of regret, a mind made of reverie. The song was already looking back in 1959, when Vee sang it with Dylan backing him on piano; now, with a greater sweep, the tune was almost generic, a folk song, something that could have come from anyone, and something that hadn't. See minnpost.com.

Nik Cohn, *Awopbopaloobop Alopbamboom — Pop from the Beginning* (1969; London: Paladin, 1972), 32, 45.

Johnny Hughes, "Elvis Presley, Buddy Holly, Joe Ely, and the Cotton Club," virtualubbock.com, January 2009.

Quarry Men, "That'll Be the Day," Philips Sound Recording Service, 1958, included on *The Beatles Anthology 1* (Capitol, 1995). With John Lowe on piano and Colin Hanton on drums.

Cathi Unsworth, *Bad Penny Blues* (London: Serpent's Tail, 2009), 95–96.

Charles Harper Webb, "The Secret History of Rock & Roll," collected in the anthology *Third Rail: The Poetry of Rock and Roll*, ed. Jonathan Wells (New York: Pocket/MTV, 2007), 156.

Paul Muldoon, "It Won't Ring True," in *The Word on the Street* (New York: Farrar, Straus and Giroux, 2013), 39.

Rolling Stones, "Not Fade Away," from *England's Newest Hitmakers!* (London, 1964). Co-produced by "Uncle Phil" Spector.

Roy Orbison, "Go! Go! Go!" (Sun, 1956).

Bob Dylan, "Bob Dylan's Blues," from *The Freewheelin' Bob Dylan* (Columbia, 1963).

Jonathan Cott, "Buddy Holly," in *The Rolling Stone Illustrated History of Rock & Roll*, ed. Jim Miller (1976; New York: Random House, 1980), 79–80.

Gerry Goffin and Carole King quoted in *The Songmakers Collection*, "The Hitmakers," directed by Morgan Neville (A&E, 2001).

The phrase "country of songs" comes from Colson Whitehead's *John Henry Days* (New York: Doubleday, 2001).

Carolyn Hester's recordings of "Wreck of the Old '97" and "Scarlet Ribbons" originally appeared on her *Scarlet Ribbons* (Coral, 1957); demo versions, with Buddy Holly on guitar, can be found on *Not Fade Away—Buddy Holly 1957: The Complete Buddy Holly* (El Toro, 2008). "Take Your Time" remains unreleased. She first recorded Holly's "Lonesome Tears"—as she sings it, a tune that sounds like both a folk song and a pop song all at once—in 1963, though it was left unissued at the time (see Hester's *Dear Companion*, Bear Family, 1995); an indelible version is on her *From These Hills* (Road Goes on Forever, 1996), a match for the smiling reading of the song she gave at the Festival della Letteratura in Mantua, Italy, in 2011, at the Teatro Bibiena, a terrifyingly steep opera house where Mozart once conducted. Along with the guitarist Bruce Langhorne and the bassist Bill Lee, Bob Dylan accompanied her on "I'll Fly Away," "Swing and Turn Jubilee," and "Come Back Baby" for *Carolyn Hester* (Columbia, 1962). Hester's producer, John Hammond, who signed Dylan to Columbia following the session, "had first seen and heard me at Carolyn Hester's apartment," Dylan wrote in *Chronicles, Volume One*. "She was going places and it didn't surprise me. Carolyn was eye catching, down-home and double barrel beautiful. That she had known and worked with Buddy Holly left no small impression on me and I liked being around her. Buddy was royalty, and I felt like she was my connection to it, to the rock-and-roll music that I'd played earlier, to that spirit" (277).

Fred Neil's pop records, including "Listen Kitten," are collected on his *Trav'lin Man: The Early Singles, 1957–1961* (Fallout). As a Brill Building writer his greatest success was Roy Orbison's searing recording of his and Beverly "Ruby" Ross's "Candy Man," the B-side of Orbison's greatest performance, "Crying" (Monument, 1961, number 2; "Candy Man" reached number 25 on its own).

Keith Richards, "Crying, Waiting, Hoping," outtake from the Rolling Stones' *Voodoo Lounge*, recorded in Dublin, November 1993, along with "Love Is Strange," Bob Dylan's "Girl from the North Country" and "John Wesley Harding," and the Beatles' "Please Please Me." Included on, among other Rolling Stones bootlegs, *Acoustic Motherfuckers*. "Buddy Holly, he could write a lick," Richards says at the end of "Crying, Waiting, Hoping." "Check him out. That motherfucker."

Cat Power, "Crying, Waiting, Hoping," from a video session recorded for rollingstone.com, posted 6 March 2007. It's Chan Marshall, perhaps alone of all the people who have taken up the song, who finds a way to sing the song past itself, past the moon-spoon wish Holly had to include in a would-be pop song in 1958: that the boy and girl would get back together. "Maybe we'll stop hoping," she sings, the words coming out slowly, all thought. "No more crying, waiting, no more hoping, that you'll come back to me."

Brian Epstein diary excerpts from Debbie Geller, *In My Life: The Brian Epstein Story* (New York: Thomas Dunne/St. Martin's,

2000), 6, 20, and *The Brian Epstein Story*, directed by Anthony Wall (BBC Arena, 2000).

Beatles, "Crying, Waiting, Hoping," Decca Records demo, 1 January 1962, available on various "Decca Audition" bootlegs.

——— "Crying, Waiting, Hoping," recorded 6 August 1963 at the BBC Paris Theatre, included on *Live at the BBC* (Capitol, 1994).

——— "Not Fade Away," "Maybe Baby," "Peggy Sue Got Married," "Crying, Waiting, Hoping," and "Mailman Bring Me No More Blues," recorded at Abbey Road studios, 29 January 1969, can be found on various Beatles bootlegs.

Pauline Kael, "The Glamour of Delinquency" (1955), collected in *I Lost It at the Movies* (Boston: Atlantic–Little, Brown, 1965), 44, and in the not-recommended posthumous collection *The Age of Movies: Selected Writings of Pauline Kael*, ed. Sanford Schwartz (New York: Library of America, 2011).

Devin McKinney, *Magic Circles: The Beatles in Dream and History* (Cambridge: Harvard University Press, 2004), 197. The best book on the Beatles.

John Lennon on "A Day in the Life," from Philip Norman, *Shout! The Beatles in Their Generation* (New York: Simon and Schuster, 1981), 290.

Jon Wiener, *Come Together: John Lennon in His Time* (1984; Urbana: University of Illinois Press, 1990). Some of the best writing on "A Day in the Life" is in Mark Shipper's novel *Paperback Writer: A New History of the Beatles*, in which a cult, the Drones, forms around the last section of the song, listening to it for hours on end. "The world record for Droning," Shipper writes, "was set by a Cherry Hill, New Jersey girl, who was called 'Drone of Ark' by her friends, until she lost all her friends" (Los Angeles: Marship, 1977), 114.

"You never use the word": John Lennon quoted in Hunter Davies, *The Beatles: The Authorized Biography* (New York: McGraw-Hill, 1968).

Manuscript of Lennon's original lyrics to "A Day in the Life" reproduced in *Bonhams Magazine*, Spring, 2006.

Jann Wenner, "B/BE/BEAT/BEATLES/BEATLES/TLE/LES/ES/S," review of *The Beatles, Rolling Stone,* 21 December 1968, 10. "I read the very first review of this record that appeared," Wenner wrote. "It was in the New York Times. In about 25 words the 'critic' dismissed the album as being neither as good as the Big Brother *Cheap Thrills* LP nor as the forthcoming Blood, Sweat and Tears album. You come up with only one of two answers about that reviewer: he is either deaf or he is evil."

Tales of Rock and Roll: Part One, Peggy Sue, directed by James Marsh (BBC Arena, first broadcast 7 April 1993).

INSTRUMENTAL BREAK:
ANOTHER HISTORY OF ROCK 'N' ROLL

The White House blues night on 21 February 2012 was broadcast as *In Performance at the White House: Red, White and Blues* (PBS, 27 February 2012).

"Robert Johnson at 100," Apollo Theater, 6 March 2012, directed by Joe Morton, produced by Steve Berkowitz, Michael Dorf, Morton, and Patricia Watt.

Robert Johnson, *King of the Delta Blues Singers* (Columbia, 1961). Issued in 2011, *The Complete Recordings: The Centennial Collection* (Sony Legacy) presented all of Johnson's surviving work, remastered with such delicacy that the songs came alive in the air, putting the listener in the room, the person singing and playing present as flesh and blood.

Bob Dylan, *Chronicles, Volume One* (New York: Simon and Schuster, 2004), 282, 285, 286.

Cat Power, "Come on in My Kitchen," from *All Tomorrow's Parties 1.1* (ATP, 2002).

Gilbert Seldes, *The Stammering Century* (1928; New York: New York Review Books, 2012), 54.

Blue Bob, "Pink Western Range," on *Blue Bob* (Solitude, 2003), lyrics by David Lynch, vocals by John Neff.

"Man, he was always": Son House to Dick Waterman quoted in Michael J. Fairchild's notes to Jimi Hendrix, *Jimi Hendrix: Blues* (MCA, 1994).

R. Crumb, "Charley Patton," collected in *R. Crumb Draws the Blues* (San Francisco: Last Gasp, 1993).

"He sold his soul": Son House to Pete Welding in Welding, "Hellhound on My Trail: Robert Johnson," collected in *down beat Music '66*, quoted in Patricia R. Schroeder, *Robert Johnson: Mythmaking and Contemporary American Culture* (Urbana: University of Illinois Press, 2004), 28. Researching his 2008 book *Delta Blues*, Ted Gioia asked the blues scholar Mack McCormick if "the time had come to put" the story of Johnson selling his soul "to rest." "McCormick vehemently disagreed," Gioia later wrote. "'When I went to New Orleans in the late 1940s to visit some record collectors,' he related, 'they told me that same story. You need to remember that almost nothing had been published on Robert Johnson at that time . . . Yet these record collectors had heard about Robert Johnson selling his soul to the Devil. I subsequently heard the same story within the black community. The fact that the same story circulated among these two groups — groups that had very little contact with each other—impressed me. It suggested that the story had deep roots, probably linking back to Johnson himself'": "Did Robert Johnson Sell His Soul to the Devil?" *Radio Silence*, no. 1, 2012, 78–79.

Henry Townsend quoted in *Can't You Hear the Wind Howl: The Life & Music of Robert Johnson*, directed by Peter Meyer (WinStar Video, 1997).

Jack White quoted in "Jack White Releases Obscure Blues Records for 'No Profit,'" *BBC News Entertainment and Arts*, 6 February 2013.

T Bone Burnett quoted in Adam Gold, "Q&A: T Bone Burnett on 'Nashville,' Elton John's Comeback and Retiring as a Producer," rollingstone.com, 18 December 2012. "And we've done that again and again and again," he added: "Johnny Cash, Hank Williams, Bob Dylan, Bruce Springsteen, Jimmie Rodgers, Howlin' Wolf, Muddy Waters." In 1981, as a struggling singer-songwriter without a label, Burnett offered his own version of the history of rock 'n' roll in the form of an invitation to a showcase performance at the Hollywood American Legion Hall:

T. BONE BURNETT
Produced:
River Deep Mountain High
Hey Jude
Oklahoma
I Who Have Nothing
El Paso

Wrote:
My Way
Night and Day
The End
Ya Ya
Bridge Over Troubled Water
Recorded:
Heartbreak Hotel
I Write the Songs
Under the Boardwalk
Strangers in the Night
Beatles at The Hollywood Bowl
ALL I ASK IS A CHANCE!

Jonathan Lethem, "The Fly in the Ointment" (2007), collected in *The Ecstasy of Influence: Nonfictions, Etc.* (New York: Doubleday, 2011), 314.

"A ghost is writing": Bob Dylan quoted in Robert Hilburn, "Rock's Enigmatic Poet Opens a Long-Private Door," *Los Angeles Times*, 4 April 2004.

Ralph Ellison, "On Bird, Birdwatching, and Jazz" (1962); collected in *Living with Music: Ralph Ellison's Writings on Jazz*, ed. Robert O'Meally (New York: Modern Library Classics, 2002).

Cuff Links, "Guided Missiles" (DooTone, 1956).

Peter Guralnick, *Feel Like Going Home: Portraits in Blues and Rock 'n' Roll* (1971; New York: Vintage, 1981), 35.

Loretha K. Smith interviewed by Grey Brennan and Steve Grauberger for "Alabama Bluesman Isaiah 'Ike' Zimmerman," Alabama Arts Radio Series, Troy University Public Radio Network, 24 July 2011.

Bob Dylan, "Love Sick" in "Angels in Venice" (Victoria's Secret, 2004). That same year, in a *60 Minutes* interview to mark the publication of *Chronicles, Volume One,* the interviewer Ed Bradley praised Dylan for his stamina: "You're still out here, doing these songs, you're still on tour." "I do," Dylan said, "but I don't take it for granted . . . It goes back to the destiny thing. I made a bargain with" (and it sounds as if the tape is cut) "it" (again the sound of a cut) "a long time ago, and I'm holding up my end." "What was your bargain?" Bradley said. "To get where I am now," Dylan said. "Should I ask who you made the bargain with?" Bradley said, grinning. Dylan snorted. "Huh," he said. "He, heh, he, you know, with. With, with, with the chief, uh, the chief commander." "On this earth?" Bradley said. "Heh, heh, on this earth and the, the other world we can't see," Dylan said.

"MONEY (THAT'S WHAT I WANT)" 1959 / 1963

"MONEY CHANGES EVERYTHING" 1978 / 1983 / 2008 / 2005

Rubella Ballet, "Money Talks" (Ubiquitous, 1985, included on *At the End of the Rainbow,* Ubiquitous, 1990).

Barrett Strong, "Money (That's What I Want)" (Anna, 1960, in Detroit, Tamla, number 23).

Raynoma Gordy Singleton, *Berry, Me, and Motown: The Untold Story* (Chicago: Contemporary, 1990), 71, 84–85. According to Larry Rohter's front-page report "For a Classic Motown Song About Money, Credit Is What He Wants," *New York Times,* 1 September 2013, Strong was responsible for the instrumental track of "Money" and was unfairly deprived of his credit both for that and for contributing to the lyrics. Seventy-two and living in a Detroit retirement home, Strong had reasserted authorship rights to

"Money," which over the years had produced millions of dollars in royalties: "Unbeknownst to Mr. Strong," Rohter wrote, "his name was removed from the copyright registration for 'Money' three years after the song was written, restored in 1987 when the copyright was renewed, then removed again the next year—literally crossed out." "The real reason Motown worked," Strong told Rohter, who also quoted Eugene Grew, the guitarist on "Money," on Strong's musical direction of the session, "was the publishing. The records were just a vehicle to get the songs out there to the public. The real money is in the publishing, and if you have the publishing"—Strong had sold his interest in the many other Motown hits he had co-written for two million dollars, which he then lost in an attempt to set up his own studio—"hang on to it. That's what it's all about. If you give it away, you're giving away your life, your legacy. Once you're gone, those songs will still be playing."

Devin McKinney, *Magic Circles: The Beatles in Dream and History* (Cambridge: Harvard University Press, 2004), 17–18.

Beatles, "Money," from *With the Beatles* (Parlophone, 1963).
—— "Money (That's What I Want)," Stockholm, 24 October 1963, included on *The Beatles Anthology 1* (Capitol, 1995).

Rolling Stones, "You Better Move On" / "Poison Ivy" / "Bye Bye Johnny" / "Money" (Decca EP, 1964).

Plastic Ono Band, "Money," from *Live Peace in Toronto, 1969* (Apple, 1969); John Lennon with Eric Clapton, guitar; Klaus Voormann, bass; and Alan White, drums.

John Lennon quoted in Jann S. Wenner, *Lennon Remembers* (1971; London: Verso, 2000), 144. From a 1971 *Rolling Stone* interview.

Brains, "Money Changes Everything" (Gray Matter, 1978).
—— "Money Changes Everything," from *The Brains* (Mer-

cury, 1980). For this rerecording of the song, Gray paused over one word, rushed over another, cueing the listener what to think; the band, or their expensive new producer, Steve Lillywhite, whose name was just too perfect, smoothed out the ham-fisted drumming of the original and steadied the beat, priming the song for the airplay it missed the first time around and never came close to touching the second. As almost always with punk, you can't remove the worst without losing what you started with — any sense of why you thought the song was worth singing in the first place. The song was too strong to clean up; it kept most of its power.

Cyndi Lauper, *She's So Unusual* (Portrait, 1983).
—— "Money Changes Everything" (Portrait, 1984, number 27).

Cyndi Lauper with Jancee Dunn, *Cyndi Lauper: A Memoir* (New York: Atria, 2012), 114.

Dock Boggs, *Country Blues* (Revenant, 1997, 1927 recordings).

Cyndi Lauper, "Money Changes Everything," from *The Body Acoustic* (Sony, 2005, CD and DVD).

Killing Them Softly, written and directed by Andrew Dominik (The Weinstein Company, 2012).

"THIS MAGIC MOMENT" 2007 / 1959

Jerry Wexler quoted in Gerri Hirshey, notes to *Till the Night Is Gone: A Tribute to Doc Pomus* (Forward/Rhino, 1995).

Lou Reed, "This Magic Moment," on *Till the Night Is Gone*. Best heard, if not in the movie, on the soundtrack to *Lost Highway* (Nothing, 1996).

Lou Reed and Ben E. King, "This Magic Moment," Prospect Park, Brooklyn, 22 July 2007.

Richard "Rabbit" Brown, "Never Let the Same Bee Sting You Twice" (Victor, 1927), can be found on the anthology *Never Let the Same Bee Sting You Twice: Blues, Ballads, Rags and Gospel in the Songster Tradition* (Document); "James Alley Blues" (Victor, 1927) is best heard on *Anthology of American Folk Music,* ed. Harry Smith (Folkways, 1952/Smithsonian Folkways, 1997).

Memphis Minnie, "He's in the Ring (Doing the Same Old Thing)" (Vocalion, 1935), is best heard on *Harry Smith's Anthology of American Folk Music Vol. 4* (Revenant, 2000).

Joe Louis, quoted in "Joe Louis Greeter at Las Vegas Hotel," United Press, carried in *Spokane Daily Chronicle,* 25 May 1955: "Former heavyweight champion Joe Louis started a new job today as official host and greeter for the Moulin Rouge, Las Vegas' first inter-racial resort hotel.

"A crowd of nearly 4000 persons filled the Moulin Rouge at its lavish opening last night.

"The new 210-room hostelry, the largest of its kind in the country, was built to accommodate Negro tourists who are barred from the 10 luxury hotels along the famed 'strip.' The $3,000,000 two-story hotel offers a swimming pool, gambling casino and theater-restaurant."

Drifters, "There Goes My Baby" (Atlantic, 1959).
—— "Dance with Me" (Atlantic, 1959).
—— "This Magic Moment" (Atlantic, 1960). All best heard on the set *Atlantic Rhythm and Blues, 1947–1974* (Atlantic, 1991).

Keith Richards with James Fox, *Life* (New York: Back Bay, 2010), 256–57.

D. H. Lawrence, *Studies in Classic American Literature* (1923; New York: Viking, 1964), 2.

Lenny Kaye, "The Second Taste, 1954–1962," in Ahmet Ertegun, *What'd I Say: The Atlantic Story* (London: A Publishing;
New York: Welcome Rain, 2001), 125.

Nan Goldin, *The Ballad of Sexual Dependency*, 1979–continuing, in the collection of the Whitney Museum of American Art
and other museums. Made entirely of still photographs, as many
as eight hundred in different versions, the music running through
it—opera, blues, soul, Top 40 hits, songs from the most fetid corners of New Wave—makes the work a movie. The music creates
the illusion of dramatic inevitability—with every cut, you feel as
if you're part of a forty-minute tracking shot. People pose happily
for occasions of ease or friendship or let's-remember-this, but in
moments of sex, misery, estrangement, or despair they don't seem
to be posing at all. There's no sense of voyeurism. Everyone is a
witness to everyone else. "Love, heroin, and chocolate" in Goldin,
The Ballad of Sexual Dependency (New York: Aperture, 1986).

Dean Martin, "Memories Are Made of This" (Capitol, 1955).

AKA Doc Pomus, directed by Peter Miller and Will Hechter
(Clear Lake Historical Productions, 2012). There is nothing re-
motely ordinary about this film. It can't be compared to any other
music biopic or documentary. There is just too much flair, and
too much love. The directors have a visual imagination that makes
the cutting together of historical footage, album covers, movie
posters, vintage interviews with the main subject, a voice-over of
Lou Reed reading Pomus's journals, talking heads of people now
looking back, still photos, and home movies seem like a revela-
tion instead of a formula. The result is countless people—Pomus's
ex-wife, his girlfriend, his children, musicians, collaborators,
friends—laughing through tears, and soon enough you're one of
them. Again and again you're pulled up short by a moment too

right to take in all at once: you hold it in your memory or stop the DVD and run it back. The most remarkable sequence comes after the end of the picture. Pomus has died. You've attended his funeral. The credits begin to roll. In a box on the right of the screen, people who you've heard tell the story are now singing or talking the words to "Save the Last Dance for Me"—and you recall the footage from Pomus's wedding, when his new wife danced with everyone but her new husband, who found a way to put it all down on paper. A phrase at a time; you're surprised how well writers can sing, or that Ben E. King, who took the lead vocal, speaks the words like talk. Five, eight, twelve, seventeen, twenty people, including, just before the end, Jerry Leiber and Mike Stoller, Leiber looking terribly debilitated and frail, but hitting all the notes—it goes on and on, until the whole song has been declaimed as if it were the Gettysburg Address.

Ray Charles, "What Would I Do Without You" (Atlantic, 1956). As Robbie Robertson hears it, a love song to heroin.

Chantels, "If You Try" (End, 1958). After "Maybe" and "I Love You So," a prototype of the life-lesson soul record—there's no hope for the singer, but you might be luckier.

Five Keys, "Dream On" (Capitol, 1959).

Lonnie Mack, "Why," from *The Wham of That Memphis Man!* (Fraternity, 1963/Ace, 2006). "A Change Is Gonna Come," "When a Man Loves a Woman," "Try a Little Tenderness," "I Never Loved a Man the Way I Love You," and even "Wish Someone Would Care" have long since become part of the pop language, but "Why" remains almost unknown. In 1963 Lonnie Mack was twenty-two, pudgy, dorky-looking despite his flattop-ducktail, but he's had two big instrumental guitar hits on a little Cincinnati label, a version of Chuck Berry's "Memphis" and "Wham!" so he gets to make an album. The last track is Mack's own "Why." The song is a staircase: after each verse, where he tells us about the woman who left him, it's the climb of the chorus to the roof, where the singer throws himself off. It's the surge of intensity, of terror—the singer terrorizing the listener, but more than that the singer terrorizing himself. It's almost inhuman, how much pain he's discovered—and the way he's discovered that he can make it real, something he can all but hold in his hands.

The first chorus comes. "Why," he sings. And then he screams the word, and it's unbearable, how far he goes with the single syllable. Mack cuts back with the next line, softly: "Why did you leave me this way." But the echo of that second "Why" is there.

Then the second verse. "Now I'm standing"—and the last word is drawn out, shuddering—"By my window/I decided"—again drawn out so far—"What I would do"—and you're sure he's going to kill himself—"I would never/Tell anybody/How much/I loved/You." And then the second chorus, the spoken "Why," then again the same word screamed, then the quiet "Why did you leave me this way"—and then something really terrible: the looming possibility that the singer might go all the way. What if he did? Would he still be standing? Would you? There is a guitar solo. It's powerful, but it's a pause, because what you're really hearing hasn't happened yet. It's what you're wishing for, what you're afraid of: the final chorus.

Do it! No, don't! Please, please, do it! No, no, no!

He brings you back into his drama, and you relax. He tells you he's writing a letter; it's stained with tears from his eyes. You can almost savor the coming repetition after the next verse: you can experience again something that you have already gotten through, stood up to, not run from. And then the levees break. Again there is the first "Why," almost crooned. Then the second, exploding as before. Then the next line, and you can feel the water rising around the singer's legs, around yours. And then, even out of this maelstrom, the shock of a long, wordless scream, a cry of anguish so extreme you have to close your eyes in shame over witnessing it, because this man is now before you, begging you to save him. And then more, farther, deeper, the now long and tangled line "You know you left me—alone and so empty" twisted into a knot that can never be undone, left behind in the wreckage of the singer's future.

"GUITAR DRAG" 2006 / 2000

Christian Marclay, "Guitar Drag" (Neon, 12-inch, 2006).

—— *Guitar Drag* (Paula Cooper Gallery video, New York, 2000).

—— *Ghost (I Don't Live Today)* (Paula Cooper Gallery video, New York, 1985).

—— "Ghost (I Don't Live Today)" (Eight & Zero 12-inch, 2007). Soundtrack to a 9 March 1985 performance.

—— *Records* (Atavistic, 1997). A collection of 1981–89 samplings, compositions, performances, radio broadcasts, and distortions, including those made from collaged LPs. With the 1981 *Guitar Drag* precursor "Phonodrum": "This piece makes use of a *phonodrum*, a primitive homemade rhythm machine," Marclay writes in the notes, before warming up and barreling off into somewhere in the middle of Monty Python's "Architect Sketch." "The mechanism consists of a short piece of guitar string taped to the tone arm as an extension of the needle, the string drags across a record or a wooden disc riddled with nails and bounces around. The vibrations are picked up by the needle and highly amplified.

The high pitch is made by using the little lever meant to switch needles from 33 to 78 RPM to scrape the record like a fingernail on a blackboard. I first used this device while playing with *The Bachelors, even*, a music/performance duo formed with guitarist Kurt Henry in 1979, when we were students at the Massachusetts College of Art in Boston. It was then that I started using records as musical instruments."

"When a record skips": Jan Estep, "Words and Music: Interview with Christian Marclay," *New Art Examiner*, September–October 2001, rpt. in Jennifer González, Kim Gordon, and Matthew Higgs, eds., *Christian Marclay* (London: Phaidon, 2005), 116.

"Bands were being formed": Scott Macaulay, "Interview with Christian Marclay," *The Kitchen Turns Twenty: A Retrospective Anthology*, ed. Lee Morrissey (New York: The Kitchen, 1992), rpt. in González, Gordon, and Higgs, *Christian Marclay*, 114–15.

"The record": Claudia Gould, "Christian Marclay" in *New Work for New Spaces* (Columbus, Ohio: Wexner Center for the Arts, 1991), rpt. in González, Gordon, and Higgs, *Christian Marclay*, 121.

"A projection": Kim Gordon, "Kim Gordon in Conversation with Christian Marclay," in González, Gordon, and Higgs, *Christian Marclay*, 20.

Quotations from Christian Marclay in 2013 are from conversations with GM.

Th Faith Healers, "Everything, All at Once, Forever," from *Imaginary Friend* (Too Pure, 1993). I've always loved the band's story that they lost the e in their The to Thee Hypnotics in a poker game. Unless it was Thee Headcoats.

Colson Whitehead, *John Henry Days* (New York: Doubleday, 2001), 265.

John Phillips, notes to *Monterey International Pop Festival* (Rhino, 1992).

Jimi Hendrix, "I Don't Live Today," from *Are You Experienced* (Track, 1967).

John Lee Hooker, "John Henry," from *The Unknown John Lee Hooker* (Flyright, 2000). Recorded in Detroit in 1949. "I don't think anyone wants to hear that old stuff today," Hooker said; among the songs he took from the air were "Jack o' Diamonds," "Two White Horses," a version of "See That My Grave Is Kept Clean," "Catfish Blues," and "Rabbit on a Log."

Jon Langford, "Lost in America," from *Goldbrick* (ROIR, 2006).

Little Richard, "Keep A Knockin'" (Specialty, 1957). Originally a fifty-seven-second fragment from the film *Mister Rock and Roll*—where Mr. Rock 'n' Roll was Alan Freed, not Little Richard —then looped by Richard's label into a two-minute, twenty-second number 8 hit after he turned his back on sinful music to serve God.

Charles Wright, "Sun-Saddled, Coke-Copping, Bad-Boozing Blues," from *Buffalo Yoga*, collected in *Third Rail: The Poetry of Rock and Roll*, ed. Jonathan Wells (New York: Pocket/MTV, 2006), 51.

American Hot Wax, directed by Floyd Mutrux, written by John Kaye (Paramount, 1978). Kaye went on to write two searingly original Los Angeles noir novels, *Stars Screaming* (New York: Atlantic Monthly Press, 1997) and, combining arcane early L.A. rock 'n' roll 45s, the death of rockabilly singer Bobby Fuller, and the Manson Family, *The Dead Circus* (New York: Atlantic Monthly

Press, 2002). Regarding the *American Hot Wax* D.A.'s "Look at that filth" at the sight of black and white teenagers in the same place, there was, in Richard Cohen's 11 November 2013 column in the *Washington Post,* a reminder that one can never afford to be smug about the supposed distance between the past and the present: "Today's GOP is not racist, as Harry Belafonte alleged about the tea party, but it is deeply troubled—about the expansion of government, about immigration, about secularism, about the mainstreaming of what used to be the avant-garde. People with conventional views must repress a gag reflex when considering the mayor-elect of New York—a white man married to a black woman and with two biracial children. (Should I mention that Bill de Blasio's wife, Chirlane McCray, used to be a lesbian?) This family represents the cultural changes that have enveloped parts—but not all—of America. To cultural conservatives, this doesn't look like their country at all." Or, presumably, his.

"TO KNOW HIM IS TO LOVE HIM"   1958 / 2006

Teddy Bears, "To Know Him Is to Love Him" (Era/Dore, 1958).

Phil Spector, *Back to Mono* (ABKCO, 1991). A four-CD set covering productions from "To Know Him Is to Love Him" to the Checkmates Ltd.'s promethean "Love Is All I Have to Give" in 1969. After mostly failed collaborations with the Beatles, Leonard Cohen, Dion, John Lennon, and the Ramones, Spector was out of the music business, a frightening legend, when in 2003 he was charged with murder in the death of Lana Clarkson. He claimed that it was an "accidental suicide" and that she "kissed the gun" he had displayed to her. Focusing often on interviews with a cool, rationally megalomaniacal Spector and on the summation by his attorney Linda Kenney Baden at Spector's first trial, in 2007, Vikram Jayanti's 2009 documentary *The Agony and the Ecstasy of Phil Spector* can leave you almost certain that Spector did not kill Clarkson; after watching his attorneys present the forensic evidence which hung the jury 10–2 for conviction, you can see Spector bringing out a gun, showing it off, listening to Clarkson talk about how worthless her life had turned out to be, and then handing it to her: *Go ahead and kill yourself, I don't care.* He was convicted in a second trial, in 2009, and in 2012 the Supreme Court refused to review the case.

Penguins, "Earth Angel (Will You Be Mine)" (DooTone, 1954). One of the first Los Angeles doo-wop singles, with Cleve Duncan singing over heavy, then skipping piano triplets as if he didn't hear them: a record that has proved as enduring as anything else America has turned up over the past sixty years, including Martin Luther King's address to the March on Washington, the legend of Sylvia Plath, or James Dean in *Rebel Without a Cause*. The song lived as true a life as in any other place or time when in 1962 Philip Roth had it hover over the pages of his first novel, *Letting Go*, finally letting it play behind what might be the saddest line he ever wrote, and this time you could imagine Cleve Duncan hearing Roth's young woman, someone, caught up in a kidnapping, for whom the song had been a receding promise that she would not always be poor, that she would not be a man's property, that someone might be nice to her: "She could not believe that her good times were all gone."

"There used to be"; "It's like when somebody dies": Jann Wenner, "Phil Spector: The Rolling Stone Interview," *Rolling Stone*, 1 November 1969, 23, 27.

"I didn't really know": Phil Spector, talk at the University of California at Berkeley, 1967.

Nik Cohn, "Phil Spector," in *The Rolling Stone Illustrated History of Rock & Roll*, ed. Jim Miller (1976; New York: Random House, 1982), 159, 152.

Shangri-Las. See the their weirdly titled collection *Myrmidons of Melodrama* (RPM, 2002, releases from 1964 to 1966), and also "Wagner versus the Shangri-Las—The Ring Cycle vs. Leader of the Pack" ("Shangri-Las: About 3 minutes long sung by babes in cool '60s clothes, pristine pop music with a producer 'Shadow Morton'—father of Rockette, son of Jelly Roll—on lead motorcycle/Wagner: 13 hours long, sung by large women with metal bras on—combines opera/heavy metal/brass bands: the three worst sorts of music in the world") in Colin B. Morton and Chuck Death, *Great Pop Things* (Portland, Ore.: Verse Chorus, 1998), 33. *The Red Bird Story* (Charly, 1991) is a four-CD set that mixes Shangri-Las recordings with singles by Bessie Banks ("Go Now"), the Ad-Libs ("The Boy from New York City"), the Dixie Cups ("Chapel of Love," the number 1 hit that put the label on the map), the Jelly Beans ("He's the Kind of Boy You Can't Forget"), Evie Sands ("Take Me for a Little While"), the Tradewinds ("New York Is a Lonely Town"—"When you're the only surfer boy around"), and actually issued 45s by Ellie Greenwich and Jeff Barry.

Far more illuminating is *Sophisticated Boom Boom: The Shadow Morton Story* (Ace, 2013), issued after Morton's death in 2013; he was seventy-two. Along with extensive and satisfying notes by Mick Patrick, it collects Morton's teenage singles, with his own thin lead singing, with the Markeys ("Hot Rod," 1958) and the Lonely Ones ("I Want My Girl," 1959), and his productions for a stunning, stripped down demo of the Shangri-Las' "Remember" (with fourteen-year-old Billy Joel on piano); Janis Ian's then-shocking interracial love story "Society's Child," from 1966; Vanilla Fudge's heroically turgid cover of the Supremes' "You Keep Me Hangin' On," from 1967; Iron Butterfly's horrifyingly influential psychedelic travesty "In-a-Gadda-da-Vida," from 1968; the New York Dolls' cover of the Cadets' 1956 "Stranded in the Jungle," from 1974; and, from 1966, Morton's own unreleased out-of-tune tone poem "Dressed in Black"—in which during a heartrendingly cynical spoken bridge, he all but confesses that his real ambition all along was less to make hit records than to become a Shangri-La himself. It was George Goldner who named him: "Before 'Leader of the Pack' came out," Patrick quotes Morton, "I did my usual—I disappeared. I did the bars on Long Island, shot some pool . . . When Goldner heard the record, he was running with it, he had to put down the credits. I had been using several different names . . . Nobody knew where to find me. Goldner said, 'Nobody knows anything about this kid. We don't know where he comes from. We don't know where he lives. He's like a shadow. As a matter of fact, I'm going to put that down on the record.' So he did, and I became Shadow Morton."

In the obituary "Yeah, Well, I Hear He's Bad . . . " the journalist David Kamp recalled a conversation with Morton in the 1990s. "He kept talking about 'the Ba-CAH-di' that did him in . . . [He] seemed especially remorseful about his behavior towards Mary Weiss, the striking lead singer of the Shangri-Las; he said the Ba-CAH-di had made him do some things to her so terrible that he didn't want to go into them"—to my mind, the kind of things George Goldner did to Arlene Smith; DavidKamp.com, 16 February 2013. Mary Weiss attended Morton's memorial. "With George everything was a chapter," she said afterward. "Now I close the book" (to GM). Shangri-La Mary Ann Ganser died in 1970 at twenty-two; her twin sister Marge Ganser died in 1996 at forty-eight.

George "Shadow" Morton, Jerry Leiber, and Mary Weiss on the Shangri-Las in "The Hitmakers" segment of *The Songmakers Collection*, directed by Morgan Neville (A&E, 2001).

"New York will never be the same": Mary Weiss, in GM, Real Life Rock Top Ten, *Salon*, 1 October 2001.

"She could not stand fame": in GM, Real Life Rock Top Ten, *Believer*, October 2011, 50.

Amy Winehouse, *Back to Black* (Island/Republic, 2006, number 2).

—— "To Know Him Is to Love Him" (2006), collected on *At the BBC* (Island/Republic, 2012), with the Arena TV documentary *Amy Winehouse: The Day She Came to Dingle*, tracing Winehouse's 2006 appearance at the Other Voices festival in the remote Irish town Dingle: with earnest interview footage throughout, a set of exquisite performances—Winehouse singing in a church, accompanied only by bass and guitar, tiny under her bouffant, dressed in black jeans, trainers, a low-cut sleeveless top, two face studs, and her tattoos.

Acknowledgments

My thanks go first to Steve Wasserman at Yale. We first met when he was a student in a class I was teaching at Berkeley (the last I would teach for almost thirty years). Soon he was in publishing, and I wrote for him when he was an op-ed editor at the *Los Angeles Times* and later when over many years he edited the *Los Angeles Times Book Review*, which he made into the best book publication in the country, and he is my editor now. At Yale I also thank John Donatich and Chris Rogers for their warmth and enthusiasm, copy editor Dan Heaton, Jay Cosgrove, Heather D'Auria, Brenda King, Ivan Lett, Jennifer Doerr, Sarah Patel, Sonia Shannon, Erica Hanson, and proofreader Jennie Kaufman. I miss the counsel of my late agent, Wendy Weil, and am deeply lucky to be able to work with Emily Forland, Marianne Merola, and Emma Patterson at Brandt and Hochman.

I thank as well Robert Polito, Luis Jaramillo, Laura Cronk, Lori Lynn Turner, and Justin Sherwood at the New School in New York; Michelle Kuo, Prudence Peiffer, Jeff Gibson,

288

and Don McMahon at *Artforum*; Vendela Vida, Sheila Heti, Andi Mudd, and Casey Jarman of the *Believer*; Dan Stone of *Radio Silence*; Melissa Harris of *Aperture*; Andrew Male, Phil Alexander, and Danny Eccleston of *Mojo*; Robert Hull at Time-Life Records; Martin Gammon of Bonhams and Butterfield; Ingrid Sischy and Graham Fuller at *Interview*; and Bill Wyman at *Salon*. For good advice, undying curiosity, inspiration, constant have-you-heards and have-you-seens, CDs, LPs, books, half-lost articles, and more, my affection and appreciation go to Anthony Allen and the Paula Cooper Gallery, Gina Basso and Rudolf Frieling of the San Francisco Museum of Modern Art, Randall Beach of the *New Haven Register*, Akeel Bilgrami, the late Adam Block, Paul Bresnick, Mary Davis, Dion, Michael Dregni, Bob Dylan's *Theme Time Radio Hour*, Pamela Esterson, Eleanor Friedberger, the late Debbie Geller, Tom Gray, Howard Hampton, Carolyn Hester, Peter Hook, Adean Kane, Doug Kroll, Cyndi Lauper, Tom Luddy, Christian Marclay, M. Mark, James Marsh, Heidi Metcalf, Jim Miller, Adam Rawls, Christopher Ricks, David Ritz, Jeff Rosen, David Ross, Al Ruppersberg, Fritz "True or False" Schneider, Dick Spottswood, Ken Tucker, Bobby Vee, Anthony Wall, Ed Ward, Lindsay Waters, Eric Weisbard and Ann Powers of the Experience Music Project Pop Conference, Mary Weiss, Jann Wenner, Howard Wuelfing, the late Tony Wilson, and Langdon Winner. I owe special thanks to Joy Baglio, Synne

Borgen, Matthew Choate, Virginia Dellenbaugh, Jordan Dependahl, Michael DeSanti, Maura Ewing, Chad Felix, Jean Garnett, Allison Kirkland, Leigh Metzler, Liz Richards, Kristin Steele, and Ida Tvedt, students in my 2012 seminar at the New School, who opened up American music to me in ways I could never have reached myself.

Some of the material here was adapted from earlier work, and I thank the publications that first let me try out themes and situations in public. "Crying, Waiting, Hoping" draws on pieces first published in *Mojo*, *Interview*, *Bonhams Magazine*, and notes to Time-Life Records' *The Folk Box*; the comments on Lonnie Mack in the notes to "This Magic Moment" from a piece in *Aperture*; the "Instrumental Break" from liner notes to *Martin Scorsese Presents the Blues: Robert Johnson* and a piece in *Artforum*; various bits and pieces were first floated by in items in my Real Life Rock Top Ten columns in *Salon* and the *Believer*.

My greatest debt is to YouTube, where almost every song, recording, performance, and movie scene mentioned in this book can be found. What I took from Jenny, Emily, Cecily, Steve, Pearl, and Rose adds up not to a debt but many smiles and much love.

Index

Note: Films are parenthetically attributed according to their reference in the text, or by director.

This page constitutes a continuation of the copyright page on p. iv.

Designed by Sonia Shannon.
Set in Electra type by Integrated Publishing Solutions.
Printed in the United States of America.

The Library of Congress has cataloged the hardcover edition as follows:
Marcus, Greil.
The history of rock 'n' roll in ten songs / Greil Marcus.
pages   cm
Includes bibliographical references and index.
ISBN 978-0-300-18737-3 (cloth : alk. paper)   1. Rock music—History
and criticism.   I. Title.   II. Title: History of rock and roll in ten songs.
ML3534.M356 2014
782.4216609—dc23
2013049423

ISBN 978-0-300-21692-9 (pbk.)

A catalogue record for this book is available from the British Library.

10 9 8 7 6 5 4 3 2 1